Young Pathfinder 4

Keep talking

et language

Other titles in the series

YPF 3
Are you sitting comfortably? Telling stories to young language learners
by Daniel Tierney and Patricia Dobson

How to keep learners spellbound and develop their listening skills in the target language at the same time. The authors provide guidelines on the type of stories that work well in the foreign language. They look at different ways of presenting stories, preparation for storytelling and follow-up activities.

YPF 2
Games and fun activities
by Cynthia Martin

Contains many strategies and enjoyable activities which enable young learners to develop their language skills. Guidance is given on choice, preparation, organisation and management of games. Support for non-foreign languages specialists is provided through examples of target language instructions for each of the activities given and an appendix of useful teacher and pupil language in French and German.

YPF 1
Catching them young
by Peter Satchwell and June de Silva

This book provides guidance on how to integrate foreign language teaching into the primary curriculum. It usggests ways of setting up and implementing a foreign language course, covering teaching aims and methodologies, resources and course content. It addresses the issue of learner progression from primary to secondary school and contains numerous ideas for classroom activities.

All CILT Publications are available from: **Grantham Book Services Ltd**
Isaac Newton Way, Alma Park Industrial Estate
Grantham, Lincs NG31 9SD
Tel: 01476 567 421.
Fax: 01476 592 393

Young Pathfinder 4

A CILT series for primary language teachers

Keep talking

Teaching in the target language

Peter Satchwell

Centre for Information
on Language Teaching and Research

The views expressed in this book are those of the author and do not necessarily represent the views of CILT.

Acknowledgements

I am indebted to Anne Farren and Catherine Cheater for enabling me to gain insight into the current primary languages projects in Richmond and Croydon. I also wish to acknowledge the thorough pioneering work of Renée Birks in *Travail d'instit'*, which has been an inspiration when working on this book.

Last, but not least, I owe a debt of gratitude to my PGCE languages students at Sussex University (1993–95) whose constant questions and lively discussion about teaching in the target language made me realise the need for more books like this one.

First published 1997
Copyright © 1997 Centre for Information on Language Teaching and Research
ISBN 1 874016 73 9

Cover by Neil Alexander
Printed in Great Britain by Bourne Press Ltd

Published by the Centre for Information on Language Teaching and Research,
20 Bedfordbury, Covent Garden, London WC2N 4LB.

Contents

Introduction

This book attempts to deal with the complex question of sustaining as much as possible of the foreign language lesson in the target language. This has implications both for the teacher and for the pupils: the teacher needs to be competent enough in the language to plan and structure his or her lessons so that there is both clear linguistic progression and constant revision for the pupils on a week to week basis; the children need to be provided with constant opportunities to use the new language for their own purposes.

Too much use of English in the foreign language lesson will undermine the children's concentration, inhibit their retention of the new phrases and slow down their language acquisition. Your pupils will only 'keep talking' in the target language if you do so!

WHY TEACH YOUNG LEARNERS IN THE TARGET LANGUAGE?

One of our main priorities should be to ensure that our pupils' first encounter with a foreign language is a positive and rewarding one. How then can we create lessons that involve children in their own learning and motivate them to become effective com-municators in the foreign language — whether with you, among themselves, or with visitors to the school?

If we can set up in the classroom experiences which involve the children . . .

- in real communication — because they **need** to say something in the new language and **want** to take part;
- in tasks which help to improve their general language skills — listening attentively, thinking about meanings, comparing their own language with the foreign language, following instructions, using dictionaries;
- in activities that introduce them to the culture and daily life of the countries where the new language is spoken;

. . . we will be giving them learning opportunities which will be memorable and useful for the rest of their lives.

If we try to define a set of realistic objectives in language learning for primary children, we can list them under four broad headings:

- communicating in the target language;
- development of language skills — mother tongue and foreign language;
- development of language learning skills;
- development of cultural awareness.

It is important to provide pupils with opportunities to be as active as possible in foreign language lessons, so that they use the new language regularly to communicate everyday needs with you and with other children and come to appreciate that it is just as effective a means of communication as their mother tongue. We can only achieve this if we provide them with the sort of learning tasks illustrated below.

Children should be given the following opportunities:

Communicating in the target language

- communicate with each other in pairs and groups as well as with the teacher;
- develop their understanding and skills through games, role play, surveys and other investigations;
- take part in imaginative and creative activities such as improvised drama, acting out stories, singing, reciting poems, etc;
- listen and respond to different kinds of spoken language;
- listen, read or view for personal interest as well as for information.

Development of language skills

- imitate pronunciation and intonation patterns;
- listen attentively to the teacher and native speakers to pick up both gist and detail;
- follow instructions and directions;
- ask about meanings, seek clarification or repetition;
- ask and answer questions and give instructions to others;
- express personal feelings and opinions;
- copy words, phrases and sentences;
- read handwriting and a variety of printed texts.

Development of language learning skills

- learn by heart phrases, rhymes, poems, tongue-twisters, songs, raps, jokes;
- acquire strategies for committing familiar language to memory;
- use dictionaries and reference materials;
- use their knowledge to experiment with language;
- understand and use informal and formal language — the use of *tu/vous, du/Sie.*

cilt

Development of cultural awareness

- work with authentic materials whenever possible: letters, magazines, newspapers, books, radio/television, from the foreign countries of the target language;
- come into contact with native speakers here and abroad;
- consider their own culture and compare it with the cultures of the target countries;
- recognise different cultural attitudes and learn the use of social conventions — forms of address, politeness, etc.

(These pupil opportunities are based on the more elaborate list as set out for KS3 and KS4 in the *Modern Foreign Languages in the National Curriculum* booklet (1995).)

Above all, we should be quite clear in our own minds as to why we need to teach in the target language for a large part of the lesson. The diagram on the following page illustrates some of the key arguments for doing so and also some of the things to watch out for in an average mixed-ability class with its usual range of children with special needs.

Non-specialist teachers often tend to assume that teaching in the target language is an 'all or nothing' situation; that any lapse from 100% use of the foreign language is somehow a cardinal sin. This is not the case. There will be many occasions in your classroom when judicious use of the mother tongue to explain something, to clarify a misunderstanding or simply to provide reassurance to an individual pupil is essential and fully justified. This policy is used all over Europe, so primary teachers need have no qualms about reverting to English to explain a grammar point, for example, or to pursue a discussion about some aspect of the foreign culture that interests the class.

Provided that you have planned say five or ten minutes of English as a regular part of your teaching strategy and that you have made clear to the children the purpose of these mother tongue 'slots' as opportunities to clear up queries and problems, no harm will be done. The sort of lesson to avoid at all costs, however, is the one in which the teacher alternates 'at the drop of a hat' from one language to the other; this just confuses everyone and reveals that the teacher has failed to set herself clear linguistic objectives from the outset.

Teaching in the target language

ADVANTAGES	KEEP A WEATHER EYE OPEN!
Enhances pupils' listening skills — makes them listen attentively.	Watch out for children who switch off and stop listening unless regularly 'prodded' and brought back into the fold.
Enhances pupils' powers of concentration.	Keep a close eye on slower pupils who soon get lost.
Introduces new sound combinations and intonation patterns.	Build into each lesson regular check-back 'slots' to make sure all have understood so far, using pupils who have understood to explain/demonstrate to those who have not.
Encourages mimicry.	
Encourages new body language and mime to express meaning.	Devise a system of regular praise and rewards for responses to listening as well as speaking tasks.
Ensures immersion in the new language for the maximum possible time, giving pupils the opportunity to assimilate the language subconsciously.	Avoid at all costs mixing English and foreign language throughout the lesson — this just confuses everyone!
Provides opportunities to carry out daily classroom routines in a new language, giving credibility and validity to the foreign language as a genuine means of communication.	Decide with the class at what point in the lesson English is allowed — and why? Some teachers have a specific weekly session in English (say ten minutes) to clear up misunderstandings, queries and worries.
Gives opportunities for total physical response in mime, gesture, actions to convey understanding of new phrases without the use of English.	Keep constant checklists of the target language phrases you plan to use and be **consistent** from week to week, ensuring that you **constantly recycle** the structures and vocabulary from previous lessons.
Provides opportunities for fun and games at a simple level, often reinforcing basic skills and concepts learnt in the mother tongue, e.g. time, numbers, months, seasons, distances.	Reinforce the words and phrases used orally with classroom display as an *aide-mémoire* for the children, using as many visuals and symbols as possible.
Gives access to a new culture through learning new rhymes, tongue-twisters, poems, songs, raps, stories.	Give complete beginners plenty of time (several weeks) to absorb the new language before you expect them to give more than one word answers. Individuals will start to produce phrases in the foreign language when they are ready and should not be forced to speak too soon.
Provides opportunities to participate in customs and festivals from another culture, e.g. birthdays, namedays, Christmas, Easter, national festivals.	

CiLT

Can I do it?

Whether you teach in a primary or a special school, it is unlikely that you will be a graduate in the foreign language you are teaching. This is not a major problem. It is not necessary to be a languages specialist to teach young beginners effectively. It is, however, essential that you are **confident in yourself** that you can master the vocabulary and structures of **the limited number of topics** that you have planned for the year and that you have a reasonable repertoire of classroom language (see Chapter 2). You will also need to be confident, of course, that the foreign language you use with the children is up to date and that your pronunciation and intonation is as accurate as possible. This may need some remedial work on your part in advance of starting to teach your class (see suggestions in YPF 1: *Catching them young,* Chapter 4).

A useful guide to the sort of skills and linguistic knowledge you need to aim for is set out in the document which forms the basis for the current Scottish primary retraining programme (*MLPS — Competences,* SOED,1994). These are the areas of competence every primary teacher of languages needs to concentrate on:

- ☑ the sound system of the language — i.e. accurate pronunciation/intonation;

- ☑ the alphabet and the numbers;

- ☑ personal language — yourself, your family, where you live;

- ☑ descriptive language — people, animals, clothes, houses, town, the environment, weather, food and drink;

- ☑ affective language — likes/dislikes, feelings, emotions, aches and pains, praise, terms of endearment;

- ☑ classroom language — daily routine, greetings, instructions, language the teacher needs for organising pupil activities, language the pupils need for asking for permission, for help, and for solving problems;

- ☑ language to cover activities from other curriculum areas such as maths, art, craft, PE, home economics, science, technology, drama, e.g.
    draw, colour, measure, cut, fold, stick . . .
    seasonal activities
    run, jump, catch, sit, stand, lie . . .
    parts of the body
    touch your . . . left/right toe . . . etc;

- ☑ language needed to:
    play games;
    teach children poems, *comptines,* songs;
    tell and act out with the children popular stories in the foreign language.

Having planned your lessons carefully and scripted the target language phrases you are going to use — and also the key phrases you are going to teach the children to use — the motto is to 'have a go' and not be afraid of making mistakes. We all get our genders, adjective endings or our word order wrong at some time or other — and it does no harm if the children realise that you are still learning too!

We hope that the following chapters will go some way to boosting your confidence in using French or German in the classroom on a regular basis and that you will be able to build and slowly expand both your own and the children's stock of useful phrases.

Bon courage . . . und viel Spaß!

1 Communication in the classroom

WHAT KIND OF LANGUAGE?

If we are not to make complete fools of ourselves when we travel abroad as adults, we need to acquire some basic **communicative competences** in the language of the country we are visiting:

- making ourselves understood, learning how to get by;
- using a dictionary or phrase book intelligently;
- saying the right things at the right time to the right person with some awareness of the appropriate greetings and politenesses; and
- ultimately coping with unpredictability and learning how to use the language creatively to keep up a conversation with native speakers.

At primary school we can only begin to build some of the foundations for these language competences, but it is important to remember that in language lessons we are always teaching other **life skills** alongside the purely linguistic. The immediate aim in the primary classroom is to get the children to see that they can use this new language to say the things they want to express by recombining the phrases and vocabulary they have learnt to create their own meanings — and that this can be enjoyable and rewarding. The long-term aim, of course, is for them one day to be able to transfer the language and the skills from the classroom to use them effectively in the real world amongst native speakers.

We need therefore to create a classroom atmosphere that is relaxed, supportive to pupils of all abilities, full of fun and above all full of action for the pupils.

> *Pupils learn through what they **do**, not through what they are told.*
> (Holmes B, *Communication re-activated*, CILT, 1991)

The implication for you the teacher is that you will need to build into your lessons a wide variety of pupil activities so that the ratio of pupil talk to teacher talk is as high as possible.

What kind of language do we need in the primary classroom? On the one hand there are all the daily interactions between teacher and pupils, involving classroom routines and organisation as well as the personal interests and enquiries of individual pupils. On the other there are all the vocabulary areas implicit in the topics the teacher has chosen for the year.

And last but not least, all those unpredictable occasions and interruptions when the teacher has to respond 'on the hoof' to events which could never be planned for. We cannot possibly cater for all eventualities and you the teacher will often have to improvise in the target language, but the diagram on the opposite page shows some of the most obvious kinds of language — and you will doubtless think of more.

TEACHER TALK

Unless you are a native speaker of French or German, you could not possibly operate yourself at the same sophisticated level of language as you normally use in English — nor would the children follow you! So we need to look for the simplest instructions, the simplest explanations, the simplest question forms using a minimum of words assisted by arms, legs, hands and facial expressions to get over the meaning we are trying to convey — and the more visual aids we can think of the better.

Let us consider some of the most commonly encountered classroom situations:

- arriving at the classroom — greetings;
- entering the room;
- organising ourselves — seating, clothing, etc;
- getting children's attention — silence!;
- taking register/dinner money, etc;
- setting the programme for the day/lesson;
- starting the lesson — organising equipment/giving out materials;
- are we sitting comfortably?;
- writing up the date/weather board/other rituals;
- recapping the last lesson;
- presenting new topic/language;
- setting up pupil activity;
- explaining again/checking that all have understood;
- monitoring progress/encouraging individuals;
- explaining rules of a game/playing game;
- changing the activity/ending the activity;
- ending lesson/packing away — saying goodbye.

You will probably need much more language than this in the course of the school week, but this at least gives us a start. You will find a list of target language phrases with variations and alternatives in Appendix 1 from which you can slowly begin to build your, and the children's, repertoire of classroom language as the year progresses.

Classroom language

WIDER WORLD BEYOND CLASSROOM

TEACHER

PUPIL

Questions to pupils
Are you feeling better today?

Questions to teacher/other pupil
What do we do next, miss?

Answers to pupils
I'll try to find out for you.

Answers to teacher
I can't find my pen.

Requests to pupils
P. can you open the window please?

Requests to teacher
Miss, can you write larger, please?

Instructions
*Listen to the cassette
and colour in the pictures.*

Coping language/seeking help
What does X mean?
How do you say XYZ miss?

Explanations
*Person A describes the
picture;*
Person B must draw it.

LESSON CONTENT

Communication tasks

Development of:
language skills
language awareness
cultural awareness

= predictable, structured
language practice

Socialising
I like your new jumper.
It's your turn.

Personal
What's your sister's name?
When's your birthday?

Descriptive
*Jackie is wearing a red
jumper and a green skirt.*

Descriptive
My cat is black and white.

Narrative
Once upon a time . . .

Narrative
*We went to my nan's at the
weekend.*

Affective
That was brilliant, Jimmy!
Oh, what a mess!

Transactional
Can you find me a red pen, please?

Affective
I hate football!
I don't feel very well.

Classroom/organisational
Time to clear up!
Pack your things away now.

Transactional
Will you lend me a pencil?

Classroom
Where's the glue gone?
Can I have the scissors, please?

= **coping with unpredictability using the foreign language in real situations**

We can begin to define a stock of phrases that encourage more interaction in the foreign language between you and your pupils if we look at other things you may need to say to groups or individuals in the course of a lesson.

TEACHER ACTIVITY

- Check that children have all the materials they need.
- Tell them where to find them.
- Give out paper/books/folders.
- Tell class how much time they have for the activity.
- Stop activity and get attention.
- Emphasise a particular point.
- Tell individuals to concentrate/behave/sit up straight/get on with work.
- Encourage children to think/guess/predict.
- Get children to read/write/draw/colour/count/recite/sing.
- Ask children to do something — stand up/draw/perform/come to the board/OHP.
- Encourage children to put hands up/reply/wait their turn.
- Set up groupwork.
- Organise team games — set ground rules!
- Start/stop!
- Express approval/surprise/delight — encourage individuals.
- Evaluate pupil performance (mime, role play) — express personal opinion/invite opinions from class.
- Suggest ideas for improvement.
- Talk about the past (yesterday/last week).
- Tell simple stories in the past.
- Talk about the future (tomorrow/next week) — when you have finished I want you to . . .

So far we have considered only the language that you the teacher may want to use. What about the children?

If they are complete beginners they will be struggling to follow what you are talking about and will be too preoccupied with trying to **understand** to be able to think about saying something themselves. As Sarah Phillips points out in *Young learners,*

> *It is almost always true that language learners understand more than they can say, and when children learn their first language they respond to language long before they learn to speak. Second language learners also have a 'silent period' in which they listen to the language around them, internalise it and formulate their own personal grammar, which they adapt and expand as they are exposed to more [of the new] language. Some authors argue that this period should be respected and that students learning a new language should not be made to speak (or write) until they are ready, that is, until they do so spontaneously.*

How then are we to ensure that they **have** understood? With beginners it is quite feasible to check understanding by asking for non-verbal responses, e.g.:

When you hear a certain number/colour, put your hand up.
Listen and draw.
Listen and do — carry out instructions or do physical activity.
Listen and make — a paper shape or model, a simple recipe.

Or, for example, if we ask them to sit down *en silence* and we have mimed our instruction clearly (sssh — *chut!*) it will soon be apparent who has not understood! Once the class has seen as a visual or a mobile they will soon make the link between the French and the English word, even though the French word sounds quite different.

En silence

The link between visuals and classroom instructions can be developed from the outset, provided that you are consistent in using the same visual to mean the same thing throughout the learning process. Once you have introduced the class to a small number of instructions with mime and actions, a lot of fun can be had by practising them together. For example:

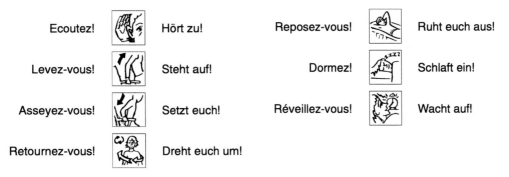

Ecoutez!		Hört zu!	Reposez-vous!		Ruht euch aus!
Levez-vous!		Steht auf!	Dormez!		Schlaft ein!
Asseyez-vous!		Setzt euch!	Réveillez-vous!		Wacht auf!
Retournez-vous!		Dreht euch um!			

Once the class has practised the actions several times you can play *Jacques a dit/ Pumpernickel sagt* (*Simon says*) which never fails with smaller children. This game can then become a regular warm-up activity at the start of lessons over several weeks. You could gradually extend the range of instructions that the children can understand. A short list of easy visuals will illustrate the point.

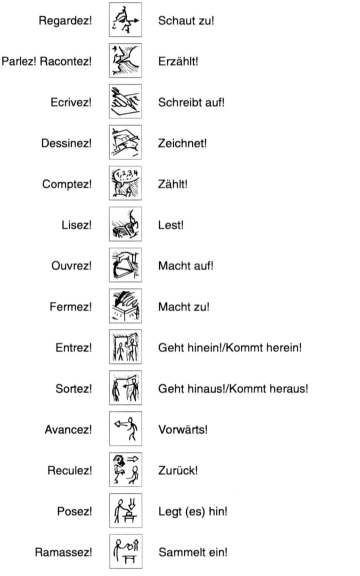

Regardez!		Schaut zu!
Parlez! Racontez!		Erzählt!
Ecrivez!		Schreibt auf!
Dessinez!		Zeichnet!
Comptez!		Zählt!
Lisez!		Lest!
Ouvrez!		Macht auf!
Fermez!		Macht zu!
Entrez!		Geht hinein!/Kommt herein!
Sortez!		Geht hinaus!/Kommt heraus!
Avancez!		Vorwärts!
Reculez!		Zurück!
Posez!		Legt (es) hin!
Ramassez!		Sammelt ein!

. . . and so on.

CiLT

As with instructions of any kind, it is possible to make up games which get the children off their seats for five or ten minutes of action and fun. With the list above you could repeat *Jacques a dit,* asking the children to mime the action, or start a team game where individuals have to carry out your instructions for real, for example:

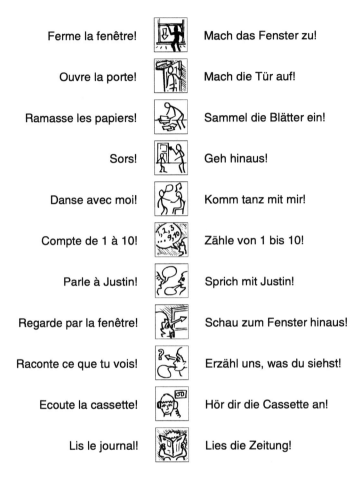

Ferme la fenêtre!		Mach das Fenster zu!
Ouvre la porte!		Mach die Tür auf!
Ramasse les papiers!		Sammel die Blätter ein!
Sors!		Geh hinaus!
Danse avec moi!		Komm tanz mit mir!
Compte de 1 à 10!		Zähle von 1 bis 10!
Parle à Justin!		Sprich mit Justin!
Regarde par la fenêtre!		Schau zum Fenster hinaus!
Raconte ce que tu vois!		Erzähl uns, was du siehst!
Ecoute la cassette!		Hör dir die Cassette an!
Lis le journal!		Lies die Zeitung!

Eventually, this can be turned into a game of charades, where teams have to guess the action and say it in the foreign language.

It is worth mentioning at this point how important it is for the teacher to try to master the distinction between the singular and plural verb forms for commands, e.g.:

assieds-toi/asseyez-vous!   *Setz dich/setzt euch!*

Whether you are teaching German or French, it is tricky not to get caught out yourself when changing from addressing the whole class/group to individuals, e.g.:

John, Alan, Keith ,	asseyez-vous!
	setzt euch!
but: *Jane,*	assieds-toi!
	setz dich!

PUPIL TALK — THEIR 'SURVIVAL KIT'

If the target language is to become the 'normal' medium for classroom interaction between you and the pupils and from pupil to pupil, the children will need to learn the phrases and expressions to cope with a range of everyday classroom situations. The language that your pupils will need initially falls into two distinct categories:

- the 'survival kit' they will need to communicate with you on an individual basis — pupil/teacher interaction;
- the language they will need to play games in a group or in pairs or to practise dialogues and role plays with a partner — pupil/pupil interaction.

For their 'survival kit' they will need to learn phrases to attract your attention and ask you questions:

Asking for . . .

. . . help

Pardon, madame! *	*Entschuldigen Sie, Frau X. **
Aidez-moi, s'il vous plaît!	*Können Sie mir bitte helfen?*
Je ne comprends pas.	*Ich verstehe nicht.*
Vous pouvez m'aider, s'il vous plaît?	*Ich brauche Hilfe!*

. . . repetition

| *Vous pouvez répéter, s'il vous plaît?* | *Wiederholen Sie, bitte!* |

. . . clarification

| *Comment ça s'écrit?* | *Wie schreibt man das?* |
| *Comment dit-on en français . . ?* | *Wie sagt man auf deutsch . . ?* |

. . . equipment

| *Je n'ai pas de feutres.* | *Ich habe keine Filzstifte.* |
| *J'ai perdu ma gomme.* | *Ich habe meinen Radiergummi verloren.* |

Asking . . .

. . . where something is

Où est la colle, svp?	*Wo ist der Klebstoff, bitte?*
Où sont les ciseaux?	*Wo sind die Scheren?*

. . . where to put something

Où est-ce que je mets la peinture, madame?	*Wo soll ich das Bild hinlegen?*

. . . permission

Pardon, madame. Je peux aller aux toilettes, s'il vous plaît?*	*[Entschuldigung.]* Darf ich bitte auf die Toilette gehen?*
Je peux emprunter une règle, s'il vous plaît?	*Darf ich bitte ein Lineal ausborgen?*
Est-ce qu'on peut tirer les rideaux/ baisser les stores, s'il vous plaît?	*Dürfen wir die Vorhänge zuziehen/die Jalousien herunterlassen, bitte?*
Je peux travailler avec N/tailler mon crayon, s'il vous plaît?	*Darf ich mit N arbeiten?/meinen Bleistift spitzen?*

*   As most children will find it hard to remember the polite phrases, especially *'Entschuldigung'* in German, you may well have to compromise at first and accept 'minimal' phrases, but you should insist that all children eventually get their tongues round the difficult words — you could have a lot of fun practising *'Entschuldigung'* as a rhythmic steam engine game!

Making apologies

Excusez-moi, madame.	*Entschuldigen Sie, Frau X.*
Pardon, madame.	
Je regrette d'être en retard.	*Verzeihung, daß ich zu spät komme.*
J'étais malade/absent.	*Ich war krank/nicht hier.*

Making complaints

Madame, je ne vois pas le tableau/ l'écran.	*Ich kann die Tafel/die Leinwand nicht sehen.*
Madame, Jenny triche!	*Frau X, Jenny mogelt!*
John a pris mon crayon.	*John hat meinen Bleistift genommen.*

Giving explanations

On coupe le papier comme ça.   *Man schneidet das Papier so.*
Puis on le déplie sur la ligne.   *Dann faltet man es auf der Linie.*

Giving excuses

J'ai oublié mon classeur.   *Ich habe meine Mappe vergessen.*
J'ai perdu le papier.   *Ich habe das Blatt verloren.*

Giving directions to others

Tu colories les animaux.   *Du malst die Tiere an.*
Tu les découpes. Tu les colles dans *Du schneidest sie aus. Du klebst sie in dein Heft.*
ton cahier.

Describing people and things

Mon ami James est petit et mince. Il *Mein Freund James ist klein und mager.*
porte un pantalon gris et un pull rouge. *Er hat eine graue Hose und einen roten Pullover an.*
Mon chat Timmy a un an. Il est orange, *Meine Katze Mitzi ist ein Jahr alt. Sie ist orange,*
noir et blanc. *schwarz und weiß.*

There will also be occasions when the children want to express their feelings and emotions and they will certainly want to express their preferences, so we need to build in opportunities to practise such phrases as:

Moi, j'aime bien les glaces.   *Ich esse gern Eis.*
J'adore le foot.   *Ich spiele sehr gern Fußball.*
Je n'aime pas les haricots —   *Bohnen mag ich nicht — ich esse lieber*
je préfère les carottes.   *Karotten.*
Je déteste les escargots.   *Schnecken mag ich gar nicht.*

THE ACTIVE CLASSROOM

If you are to create a really active classroom in which the pupils are doing just as much work as you are, you will need to think of a wide range of activities that require the pupils to speak to each other, not just to you.

Pairwork and role play, team games and board or card games therefore need to become regular features of your lessons. But we cannot expect these pupil/pupil activities to succeed unless we first teach the children the phrases that they will need to interact with

CiLT

each other in the target language. If we fail to do this the inevitable result is that the children constantly drop back into English the moment your back is turned.

For role play tasks, pupils will need, for example:

Tu es A, je suis B.	*Du bist A, ich bin B.*
Tu commences/je commence.	*Du beginnst/ich beginne.*
C'est à toi.	*Du bist dran.*
Madame/Maîtresse, nous avons fini!	*Frau X, wir sind fertig!*

In order to play games the children will need such phrases as:

C'est à moi.	*Ich bin dran.*
C'est mon tour.	*Jetzt komme ich dran.*
Paul, tu as Monsieur B, le boulanger?	*Paul, hast du Herrn B, den Bäcker?*
Attends! Un moment!	*Warte! Moment mal!*
Tu triches! Ne triche pas!	*Du mogelst! Du sollst nicht schwindeln!*
Avance/recule de 2 cases.	*2 Felder vorwärts/zurück.*
Passe un tour.	*Einmal aussetzen.*

. . . and so on.

(A fuller list of such phrases is included in Appendix 1 and at the back of YPF2: *Games and fun activities* by Cynthia Martin.)

One way of presenting these phrases to the class is obviously for you to play a demonstration game on the board or OHP with one of the pupils — or with a native speaker parent or a foreign language assistant (FLA), if you are lucky enough to have one! Once this demonstration game has been played, you will have to find some way of providing the children with *aides-mémoire* if they are to use the phrases among themselves. You will have to rehearse the phrases with the whole class until you are satisfied that they all understand and can pronounce them reasonably accurately. You might even try adding gestures/body language to go with each phrase — and if you can't think of any, your class certainly will! You could also display this week's new phrases on the wall with visuals wherever possible.

This will take time, but if you persist in praising children who use the phrases well and you make a point of revising them every week, the class will soon use them with confidence and enjoy playing games in the new language.

TOTAL PHYSICAL RESPONSE

In aiming to provide maximum pupil activity in the target language, you need to be aware of the enormous potential of total physical response (TPR) — a technique used all over Europe. The teaching and learning of new vocabulary areas is greatly enhanced if the pupils are encouraged to move physically in response to instructions, descriptions and stories told in the target language. The best-known TPR activities are probably action songs, such as *Head and shoulders, knees and toes,* the *Hokey Cokey* or *Alouette.* And of course the game of *Simon says* requires a total physical, non-verbal response:

> *Jacques a dit: Touche la tête/la bouche/le pied . . .*
> *Pumpernickel sagt: Zeig mir die Nase/die Hand/den Daumen . . .*

This technique can be be transferred to all sorts of other vocabulary areas and classroom situations. When teaching classroom instructions, the class can play team games where they have to race to carry out the task:

> *Ferme la porte!*   *Mach die Tür zu!*
> *Ouvre la fenêtre!*   *Mach das Fenster auf!*
> *Allume la lumière!*   *Mach das Licht an!*
> *Essuie le tableau!*   *Wisch die Tafel ab!*

. . . and so on.

Or you can adapt party games to have teams competing in different ways:

> *Apporte-moi . . . une gomme/une trousse/un crayon, . . .*
> *Bring mir . . . einen Radierer/einen Bleistiftspitzer/einen Kugelschreiber . . .*

A lot of fun can be derived from 'nonsense' games where you challenge the class to carry out your instructions:

> *Pose ton cahier sur ta chaise,*   *Leg dein Heft auf deinen Stuhl,*
> *pose ta gomme sur le cahier,*   *leg deinen Radiergummi aufs Heft,*
> *pose ton crayon sur ta tête,*   *leg deinen Bleistift auf deinen Kopf,*
> *assieds-toi,*   *setz dich hin,*
> *lève la main gauche,*   *heb die linke Hand,*
> *lève-toi . . .*   *steh auf . . .*

This can be developed to include more complex instructions such as:

Paul, tu te poses près d'une fille qui porte un ruban vert/une jupe bleue/des lunettes/qui a une trousse rouge . . .

Paul, du stellst dich neben ein Mädchen, das ein grünes Haarband/einen blauen Rock/ eine Brille trägt/eine rote Federmappe hat . . .

Another way of using TPR is to invite pupils to stand up, clap or mime in response to your questions:

Si tu aimes les bananes/les glaces, mange une! (Mime)
Si tu sais nager/faire du vélo, montre-nous!
Si tu as des frères, bats des mains/claque des doigts!
Si c'est aujourd'hui ton anniversaire/ta fête, lève-toi!

Wenn du gern Eis/Bananen ißt, iß eins/eine!
Wenn du schwimmen/radfahren kannst, zeig uns!
Wenn du Brüder hast, klatsch in die Hände/schnips mit den Fingern!
Wenn du heute Geburtstag/Namenstag hast, steh auf!

TPR can equally well be applied to storytelling. A well-known children's story (*Goldilocks, Pied Piper, The very hungry caterpillar,* etc), told in a simplified version in the target language, can be introduced with large visuals of the main characters, events or places on the board/OHP and the children are invited to invent their own mimes to accompany those key events/characters. Each time they hear them, as you narrate the story, the children mime the action and are thus drawn into the story even though they will not understand every word. An example from *Goldilocks* might be:

Boucle d'Or pousse la porte et entre sur la pointe des pieds.
Elle a faim.
Elle goûte la soupe d'une grande assiette. Aïe, c'est chaud!
Quelqu'un a goûté ma soupe, dit le gros ours.
Quelqu'un est couché dans mon lit, dit le petit ours.

Further TPR ideas can be found in *Young learners* by Sarah Phillips and in many EFL materials produced for teaching English abroad.

An invaluable teaching aid is the use of puppets in language lessons. These can be simple finger puppets or more sophisticated glove puppets with a personality of their own.

Experiments in Germany, France and Italy have proved that the use of a puppet (or even a soft toy animal) will often catch the imagination of small children and encourage them to speak a new language because their shyness is overcome by their involvement with a new 'personality' in the classroom.

The puppet becomes the centre of attraction and allows the teacher to retreat from centre stage as the children start to communicate with the puppet as a non-threatening person who will not tell them off or correct their mistakes. The puppet arouses an irresistible sense of curiosity, a desire to touch him or her and of course a great sense of fun!

A puppet can adopt all sorts of characteristics, depending on the histrionic talents and imagination of the teacher. He can:

- talk to the teacher;
- talk to the whole class;
- talk to and touch individual children;
- make mistakes;
- get up to mischief, show off;
- be sad, happy, play tricks on the teacher and the class;
- be told off by the teacher, get into scrapes of all kinds;
- always be the children's friend and confidant, whispering the correct answer to pupils who get stuck;
- also be the ring leader for pupil activities, showing them what to do or demonstrating how to play a game.

In short, the puppet becomes the teacher's 'stooge' — and, of course, **the puppet never, ever speaks a word of English!!**

Examples of the use of a glove puppet as a key figure in the methodology can be found in two commercially produced primary courses:

Wer? Wie? Was? 1 (GILDE Verlag) assumes that the teacher will use **Tanja**, a girl puppet with blond pigtails, to do most of the oral practice in class — and teachers using the materials report that pupils are very disappointed if Tanja does not appear in every lesson.

In **Gaston 1,2,3** (ELI) the mustachioed glove puppet **Gaston** is both a key figure in the pupils' book cartoon strips and a constant physical presence in the classroom, to present new language, remind the children of what they already know and create a focal point for spontaneous dialogue. The puppet can, of course, be a constant help in practising correct pronunciation and intonation and he can assist children with the first steps in reading the printed word.

READING AND WRITING

SEEING THE PRINTED WORD

All the evidence from primary schools in the UK and the rest of Europe points to the distinct advantages of relating the spoken to the printed word from quite an early stage. Of course we must not abandon the golden rule of extensive and thorough oral practice to establish correct pronunciation and intonation **before** we show the children the new words in print. But withholding the written form of the language for too long tends to inhibit the children's natural curiosity and may well hold up the learning process. We all need 'hooks' to hang new words and phrases on, and for most children it is probably helpful to associate the printed word with visuals wherever possible, so that the recall of its sound is prompted by the symbol/picture without forcing the child to rely solely on 'reading' the word. We need therefore to think carefully about what stimuli will help children to memorise the phrases we have been trying to teach them and to devise ways of providing *aides-mémoire* on a daily basis through various forms of display.

Although reading is not a priority with infants, we should be consciously building up reading skills as the children progress through the junior school. By the time they are nine or ten they should be quite capable of working their way through simple graded readers of cartoon stories such as *Bibliobus, Lesekiste* (MGP) or *L'album des monstres* (LCP).

CREATING A CLASS PICTORIAL DICTIONARY

At some point quite early on the children will need to learn the alphabet and the names of the most common classroom objects — especially their own personal belongings: pens, pencils, books, clothing, furniture, etc.

It is advisable to teach the class only a small number of new words each week, depending on age, ability and their stage of development.

Children of eight and over may well benefit from creating their own class 'Pictionary', in which they build their own collection box of new words with visuals. The children illustrate the word with a picture and sort it into a colour-coded cardboard box by gender (*le,la,l'*) (*der, die, das*), by topic and/or alphabetical order. This home-made picture dictionary eventually becomes accessible for any child who has forgotten a word to go and look it up.

Obviously it helps children to memorise the classroom objects if they are all clearly labelled. Some primary classrooms have virtually every piece of furniture and equipment labelled and colour-coded by gender: *la table* in red, *le rétroprojecteur* and *l'ordinateur* in blue. In German a third colour has to be found for neuter words: *das Fenster*. This is a task that the pupils can well do for you, using a simple word-processing package. Large lettering in solid black can easily be highlighted in colour to identify gender.

WORKSHEETS

Simple worksheets can be devised as reinforcement at almost any stage, but you will be the judge of what is appropriate for your class and of the level of language they can cope with. Children can be asked to copywrite and match or join the words to pictures of the five to ten new objects they have learnt this week (see example on pp24–25).

Or they can work orally in pairs: A is blindfolded, B holds one of the objects, A has to guess what it is:

> *C'est une gomme? Non. C'est une trousse? Oui.*
> *Ist es ein Radiergummi? Nein. Ist es eine Federtasche? Ja.*

They can also be asked
to draw:

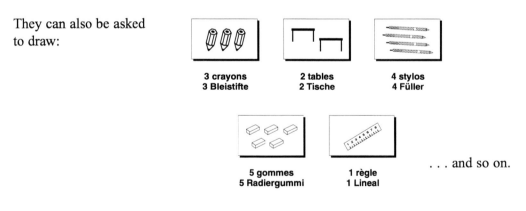

3 crayons 3 Bleistifte	2 tables 2 Tische	4 stylos 4 Füller
5 gommes 5 Radiergummi	1 règle 1 Lineal	

. . . and so on.

You will have your own ideas of the kind of worksheets that work for your particular class. Many can be devised in the target language based on what your pupils can do in their mother tongue in other areas of the curriculum. You will find a very helpful collection of excellent ideas in *Jeux faciles* and *Superspiele,* photocopiable sets of worksheets by Clare Cooke, published by Language Centre Publications. These are all very accessible to primary children. You will also find useful and rewarding the many domino and dice games in the Miniflashcards catalogue (see Resources section in Appendix 3).

Once you have acquired a small stock of simple rubrics and instructions for worksheets in French/German, you can cover most eventualities. For example:

Cherche Wally/les animaux/monsieur X		Suche Wally/die Tiere/Herrn X
Trouve les mots cachés		Suche die versteckten Wörter
Ecris la liste		Schreib die Liste
Où est le fantôme?		Wo ist der Geist?
Qui est-ce?		Wer ist das?
Regarde le plan/l'image		Sieh dir den Plan/das Bild an
Colorie (l'arc-en-ciel, les animaux)		Male (den Regenbogen/die Tiere) an
Dessine		Zeichne
Découpe l'image		Schneide das Bild aus
Relie (les mots et les images)		Verbinde (Wort mit Bild)
Complète les images/les boîtes		Ergänze die Bilder/die Felder
Coupe		Schneide
Plie		Falte
Colle		Klebe
Attache		Hefte

. . . and so on.

Example worksheet

Relie
Verbinde

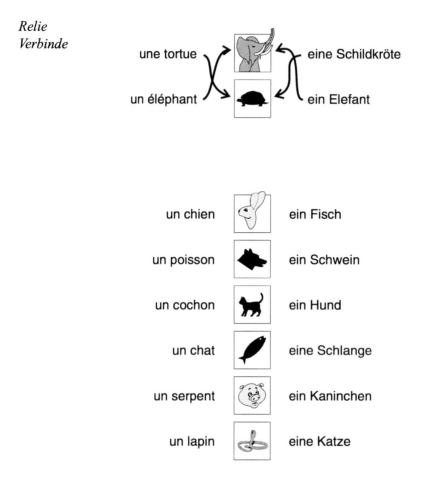

une tortue — eine Schildkröte

un éléphant — ein Elefant

un chien — ein Fisch

un poisson — ein Schwein

un cochon — ein Hund

un chat — eine Schlange

un serpent — ein Kaninchen

un lapin — eine Katze

Dessine et colorie
Zeichne und male an

un chat noir une tortue brune un serpent vert
eine schwarze Katze eine braune Schildkröte eine grüne Schlange

CiLT

Cherche les animaux. Dessine-les.
Suche die Tiere. Zeichne sie.

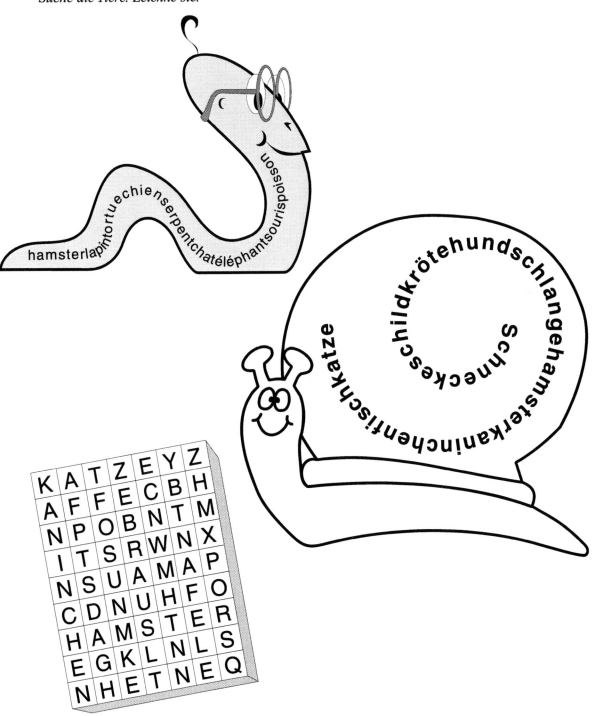

2 Progression

It is essential that primary teachers plan for progression in the foreign language and map out for themselves a very structured approach to their teaching, whether they are teaching the language for just one year or over two or more years. Simply stringing together a series of unconnected games and activities which will entertain and amuse the children is not sufficient, even with the four- and five-year-olds. If she is to ensure real and measurable progress by all of the children in her charge, the teacher must devise a structured 'course' for herself; a sequence of activities which build one upon the other and ensure that key phrases learnt at the beginning of the year are constantly recycled and revisited in later units of work so that the pupils do not forget them. There needs to be progression both in terms of learning and social skills as well as linguistic skills.

It helps to have built into the programme some measurable 'waystages' that demonstrate to the learners (and their parents) that they really have achieved something. These waystages do not need to be old-fashioned pencil and paper 'tests'. There are many ways in which primary children can show what they can do and the most rewarding are the opportunities to **perform** in the foreign language. Whether it be a poem or a rap, a concert including songs and dances from the foreign country, recitation of rhymes, tongue-twisters, or acting out their own version of a well-known story, a simple playlet that they have created with costumes and props, the children will enter into the performance with gusto — and these will be the events that they remember later in life. There is also plenty of scope for them to celebrate their achievements in the foreign language in other forms: they can display collages, models and artwork labelled in the language, cartoon characters and puppets from foreign language stories they have heard or read can appear around the school, even multi-lingual signposts can be made to welcome visitors (see Chapter 3).

By sitting down to plan your target language activities and scripting the key phrases that you wish to teach the children to use themselves as well as the ones you want them to understand, you will quickly identify your own strengths and weaknesses in the foreign language. This planning process will help you to stay in control of the language you are going to use in the classroom and to some extent define the limits of the vocabulary you are able to use, although of course you will have on occasions to consult native speakers and a dictionary when embarking on a topic you have never taught before! The clue is to start small and gradually build up your repertoire — and the children's — as your confidence grows.

In view of the lack of research into young children's language learning the **notional model of progression** which follows is offered as a tentative one which you the teacher will need to modify in the light of your experience with your pupils and your own school circumstances. If it proves a useful starting point, it will have served its purpose.

It is based on an 'ideal' scenario where pupils start learning the foreign language at five or six and continue throughout the junior school for a further three or four years. In an attempt to simplify what is a very complex issue, this model is divided into two rough age categories: INFANTS and JUNIORS.

Our expectations of four- to six-year-olds will obviously need to be simpler and far less sophisticated than the demands we might make (including reading and writing) on the seven- to ten-year-olds. The starting point is therefore a small 'core' of target language for the really young beginners which can serve as the foundation blocks upon which to build as the children mature. The second section suggests ways in which you might expand this 'core' to include progressively more sophisticated language and ideas, extending into longer and more complex phrases which older juniors should find challenging to understand and rewarding to learn.

INFANTS: 4–6

LISTENING

The receptive listening skills may need to be built up over several months before many of the children feel able and confident to attempt to produce any of the target language for themselves. The more often we can expose them to the new language the better, even if it is only five or ten minutes a day.

SPEAKING

Slowly but surely individual children will begin to mimic the words and phrases of the teacher (or the puppet!) in their own time. This is a stage that should not be forced; some of the shyer children will not come out of their shell for some time!

Productive speaking skills come slowly. Initially one-word answers: *oui, non/ja, nein,* or the name of an object or person: *crayon, chat, Gaston/Lineal, Hund, Tanja,* are all that we should expect.

Slowly these can be built up into short phrases with which the children can answer the teacher's questions:

Je m'appelle X.	*Ich heiße X.*
(J'ai) 6 ans.	*(Ich bin) 6 (Jahre alt).*
(J'ai) un chat.	*(Ich habe) eine Katze.*

It is the teacher's task to ensure a progressive build up of more key phrases, introducing a few new ones with each topic, or perhaps two or three each week, e.g.:

J'habite à . . .	*Ich wohne in . . .*
J'ai deux soeurs et un frère.	*Ich habe zwei Schwestern und einen Bruder.*
Mon frère s'appelle . . .	*Mein Bruder heißt . . .*
Mon chien s'appelle . . .	*Mein Hund heißt . . .*

Simultaneously, with word recognition (animals, classroom objects, etc) we need to expand the children's repertoire of usable productive phrases that enable them to communicate in the target language in class, both with you and with each other: the gradual enhancement of classroom interaction needs to be a deliberate part of our strategy. This can only be done if we consciously choose the **building blocks** of language we want the children to learn to use for themselves.

P/T language

Excusez-moi, madame . . .	*Entschuldigen Sie, Frau X . . .*
Pardon, madame . . .	*Verzeihung.*
Je peux aller aux toilettes, svp?	*Darf ich bitte auf die Toilette gehen?*
Où est la colle, svp?	*Wo ist der Klebstoff bitte?*
On peut ouvrir la fenêtre, svp?	*Dürfen wir das Fenster aufmachen, bitte?*
Je n'ai pas de . . . crayon, papier.	*Ich habe kein Papier/keinen Bleistift.*

P/P language

Tu as un animal?	*Hast du ein Haustier?*
Quel âge as-tu?	*Wie alt bist du?*
Tu habites où?	*Wo wohnst du?*
Qui est-ce? (pointing to a photo)	*Wer ist das?*
Où est ma gomme?	*Wo ist mein Radierer?*

---

cilt

From this stage we can progress to adding descriptive language, putting adjectives with nouns:

C'est un serpent > c'est un serpent vert et jaune.
J'ai un chien > j'ai un petit chien noir et blanc.
J'ai un lapin > j'ai un grand lapin qui aime les carottes.

Das ist eine Schlange > eine grüngelbe Schlange.
Ich habe einen Hund > einen kleinen, schwarzweißen Hund.
Ich habe ein Kaninchen > Ich habe ein großes Kaninchen, das gern Karotten frißt.

This process can eventually lead to a point where even infants are able to draw pictures and add simple captions of their own choice. This is simple copywriting based on a teacher's model:

Voilà mon chaton, Tiger.
Il est noir, blanc et orange.
Il a six mois.
Il mange du Wiskas.

Hier ist mein Kätzchen, Tiger.
Es ist schwarz, weiß, orange.
Es ist sechs Monate alt.
Es frißt gern Wiskas.

After one or two years children should have acquired, within a limited range of topic areas, a fairly broad **receptive vocabulary and good understanding** of:

- teacher's instructions;
- classroom objects;
- personal descriptions of family members and friends;
- simple dialogues;
- simple games, songs, *comptines,* stories.

They should have a **productive ability** to ask and answer simple questions about:

- themselves, their family, their pets and toys;
- their likes and dislikes;

and they should be able to interact with the teacher:

- follow directions;
- ask for help;
- ask for permission;
- ask where something is.

Many children will also be able to make up very simple dialogues of their own, role playing with soft toys or puppets, for example.

They should also have a **receptive ability** to **recognise key words** and short phrases **in print:**

- days, months, colours, numbers, dates, birthdays, animals/pets
- basic instructions, e.g. *colorie, dessine, découpe, cherche . . .*
            male an, zeichne, schneide aus, suche . . .

JUNIORS: 7–10

With an increase in general learning skills across the curriculum, pupil tasks can be made progressively more challenging to include all four language skills: listening, speaking, reading and writing.

Receptive listening skills can be stretched with an expansion of story telling, both by the teacher and on cassette, by exposure to a wider variety of foreign voices on audio and video cassettes. To the listening skills can be added the **reading skills** if pupils are introduced gradually to longer sentences, short descriptive paragraphs and eventually to simple cartoon readers that they can read for pleasure at their own speed (e.g. *Bibliobus, Album des monstres, Lesekiste).*

Progression can also be ensured by widening the variety and style of texts heard and read through the introduction of a multi-media approach. Children should become familiar with video, with word processing in the target language and ultimately with CD-ROM packages.

The **productive skill of speaking** can be reinforced by simple writing tasks. In addition to longer sentences and more sophisticated dialogues and role plays, pupils will need to be challenged to initiate conversations themselves, encouraging them to recombine learnt phrases to make up dialogue for their own purposes. They can ask you or each other questions in class surveys, for example, and perhaps note the answers graphically or in writing. You may go further to include tasks which require the children to:

- record a personal profile in speech (cassette) and in writing;
- compile (over a year) a dossier/book: *Moi* or *Ich über mich,* in which the pupil writes and illustrates everything he can in the target language about his home, family, home town, friends, pets, hobbies, etc (cf *Me,* Gyles Brandreth, Knight Books, Hodder, 1979) (this is a subtle way of getting children to record their own progress);

CiLT

- produce creative and fantasy artwork with a target language text, e.g. make a 'monster' story book or cartoon strip for younger children;
- create their own card or board game with rules in the target language;
- prepare performances in the target language for parents/governors, another class or school.

Or you may decide to:

- create more sophisticated (and differentiated) worksheets which present both a challenge to the more able and offer reinforcement and support to the less able pupils in the form of puzzles, wordsearches, gap-fillers, crosswords, matching, drawing, making and doing tasks;
- establish a partnership with a primary school abroad to create penfriend correspondence on cassette, video or written, exchange of parcels, learning materials, leading ultimately to exchange visits of pupils and staff.

Help in finding a partner school abroad can be obtained from the Schools Unit at the Central Bureau (see Appendix 4) or through your local town twinning links.

There is a small number of broad topic areas that most primary language teachers and publishers have come to regard as appropriate for young beginners. You could well add others of your own.

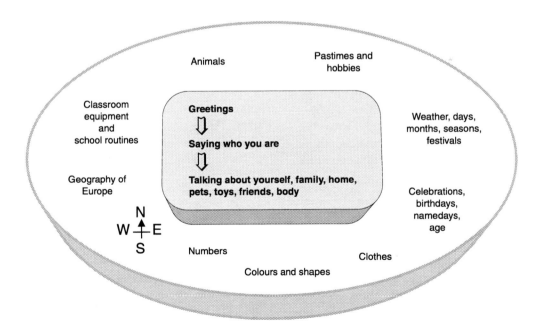

The following examples attempt to show how a core of simple basic phrases, appropriate for the youngest learners in the infants, can later be revisited and extended to present new challenges and more sophisticated tasks for children who have reached the junior school.

GREETINGS

BASIC

Bonjour! Salut! Ça va?	🤝	Guten Morgen! Guten Tag! Wie geht's?
Ça va bien, merci.	😊	Gut, danke!
Comme ci, comme ça.	😐	Es geht.
Ça ne va pas.	🙁	Nicht so gut.
Au revoir!	👋	Auf Wiedersehen!
A demain! A bientôt!		Tschüß! Bis morgen!

These basic greetings should be practised with accompanying gestures, e.g. shaking hands is an important part of both French and German culture even amongst primary age children that our children need to be made aware of. The phrases can be displayed as mobiles or on classroom walls with large visuals to show their meaning (see Chapter 3).

Musical teachers could encourage the class to make up a simple melody to sing the greetings, as long as care is taken to find the appropriate rhythms and reflect French/German intonation patterns, e.g.:

Bonjour! Ça va? Ça va bien, mer-ci.   Comme ci, comme ça.   Ça ne va pas!

Guten Morgen, wie geht's? Danke, gut! Und dir?   Es geht. Und dir?   Nicht so gut! Und dir?

EXTENSION

As pupils get older, a lot of fun can be had if children are encouraged to make their own *'Stimmungsthermometer'* (mood thermometer) as illustrated below, giving them greater scope to express their personal feelings from day to day.

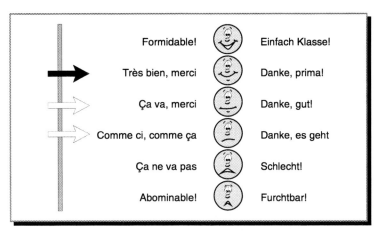

Formidable!		Einfach Klasse!
Très bien, merci		Danke, prima!
Ça va, merci		Danke, gut!
Comme ci, comme ça		Danke, es geht
Ça ne va pas		Schlecht!
Abominable!		Furchtbar!

To this can be added expressions of sympathy or surprise and eventually the pupils can be made aware of the distinction between child/child and child/adult forms of address:

Ça va?   *Wie geht's?*
Très bien, merci. Et toi/vous?   *Gut, danke. Und dir/Ihnen?*

The class can gradually acquire other sociable phrases such as:

A demain. Bon weekend!   *Bis morgen. Schönes Wochenende!*

and eventually ask about things that have just happened:

Vous avez passé un bon weekend? Où avez-vous passé les vacances?
Wie war das Wochenende? Wo waren Sie in den Ferien?

INTRODUCTIONS AND NAMES

BASIC

There are numerous ways of getting children to introduce themselves. Once you have started the ball rolling by pointing to yourself and saying: *Je m'appelle [Jean], Comment tu t'appelles?* (pointing to child), children will slowly but surely begin to get their ear and tongue round the phrase. But they will need a lot of practice until they are confident and reasonably accurate, so you could try simple rhymes like these:

> *Comment tu t'appelles?*
> *Je m'appelle Gisèle.*
> *Comment ça <u>va</u>?*
> *Ça <u>va</u>, merci, ça <u>va</u>.* [Variation: *Comme ci, comme ça*]
> OR: *Pas mal. Ça va.*
> OR: *Oh, ça ne va pas!*

It is important to get the children saying the rhyme **rhythmically,** with the emphasis carefully placed on the correct syllables. Once this is secure you can progress to *il* and *elle:*

> *Comment s'appelle-t-il? Il s'appelle Michel.*
> *Comment s'appelle-t-elle? Elle s'appelle Rachel.*
> *Et comment s'appelle-t-il?* OR: *Et lui? Et lui?* OR: *Et elle? Et elle?*
> *Il s'appelle Emile. Elle s'appelle Estelle.*

Similarly in German you can experiment with simple rhymes like this:

Guten Tag, wie heißt du?
Ich bin Anna, und wie heißt du?
Ich bin Stefan. Wie alt bist du?
Ich bin acht. Und du? Und du?

Wie heißt du?
Ich heiße Fritz.
Und wie heißt dein Hund?
Er heißt Spitz.

Ich bin Frank, und wer seid ihr?
Wie heißt sie und wie heißt er?
Er heißt Peter und sie heißt Anne,
Ich bin Axel — jetzt bist **du** dran!

Eventually the children can be encouraged to make up their own. You will find many other rhymes and songs in published materials from France and Germany; the first two rhymes above are spoken beautifully by young French children on the *Trampoline 1* cassettes, and *Anna, Schmidt & Oskar* has this simple song (on video and audio cassette) which passes round the class from pupil to pupil:

```
(sung)  Ich bin ich
        und du bist du.
        Ich heiße Helga
        und wie heißt du?        [Spoken: Ich heiße Andreas.]

(sung)  Ich bin ich
        und du bist du.
        Ich heiße Andreas
        und wie heißt du?        [Spoken: Ich heiße Brigitte.] usw
```

To introduce more action, you can use the softball game, throwing the ball to each pupil as you ask his or her name. He or she then throws it to another pupil who has to reply to his question. In this way you can ensure that all pupils have said their names — or any other phrase you need to practise.

You can rapidly build this into your daily routine by calling the register in the target language:

> *Attention! Je fais l'appel . . . Christine . . . Présente . . .*
> *Jill . . . Oui, madame./Absente, madame. Elle est malade.*
> *Seid ihr alle hier? Paßt auf! Christopher . . . Hier. Annette . . . Fehlt/sie ist krank . . .*

EXTENSION

The register call can gradually expand to include further repartee:

> *Sylvie est absente? Où est-elle?*
> *Elle est malade/chez le dentiste/chez la directrice/chez le coiffeur . . .*
> *Wo ist Sylvia heute? Ist sie krank?*
> *Sie ist beim Arzt/beim Direktor/beim Augenarzt/bei ihrer Oma . . .*

A later development involving reading and writing can be the production of a small identity card or passport:

```
┌──────────────────────────────────┐   ┌──────────────────────────────────┐
│                      ┌─────────┐  │   │                      ┌─────────┐  │
│  CARTE D'IDENTITE    │         │  │   │  AUSWEIS             │         │  │
│                      │         │  │   │                      │         │  │
│                      └─────────┘  │   │                      └─────────┘  │
│                                   │   │                                   │
│  Nom de famille: ...............  │   │  Familienname: .................  │
│                                   │   │                                   │
│  Prénoms: ....................... │   │  Vornamen: .....................  │
│                                   │   │                                   │
│  Nationalité: ................... │   │  Nationalität: .................  │
│                                   │   │                                   │
│  Date de naissance: ............. │   │  Geburtsdatum: .................  │
│                                   │   │                                   │
│  Lieu de naissance: ............. │   │  Geburtsort: ...................  │
│                                   │   │                                   │
│  Domicile: ...................... │   │  Wohnort: ......................  │
│                                   │   │                                   │
└──────────────────────────────────┘   └──────────────────────────────────┘
```

Or a less serious version could be produced if the children are encouraged to make up fictitious characters for themselves as in this example from *Schatzkiste:*

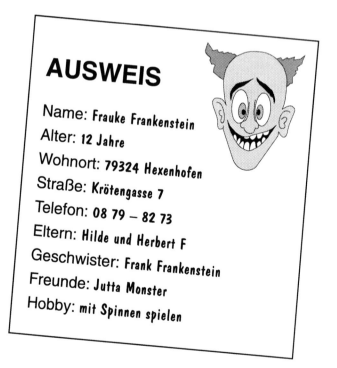

AUSWEIS

Name: Frauke Frankenstein
Alter: 12 Jahre
Wohnort: 79324 Hexenhofen
Straße: Krötengasse 7
Telefon: 08 79 – 82 73
Eltern: Hilde und Herbert F
Geschwister: Frank Frankenstein
Freunde: Jutta Monster
Hobby: mit Spinnen spielen

A simple little song like *Meine Familie* might be used to introduce the members of the family before moving on to an illustrated version with writing:

Mein Vater heißt Hans, mein Opa heißt Franz, meine Mutter heißt Renate, meine Schwester Be -

- ate. Meine Oma heißt Ottilie, das ist meine Familie. Ich heiße Fritz und mein Hund, der heißt Spitz.

Pupils will also be able to draw their family tree and label it, including if they wish photos or their drawings of family members; they could then add it to a personal dossier of the kind suggested on p30:

mamy
Oma B

pépé
Opa S

mémé
Oma S

papy
Opa B

papa
Vati

maman
Mutti

moi
ich

THE ALPHABET

BASIC

The foreign alphabet will need to be introduced a few letters at a time and the methods you use will depend very much on the maturity of the class. The stage at which you decide to practise saying the letters in the foreign language must also be your choice, but the same techniques that are used in English can also be applied here. Some teachers may opt for attaching letters to French/German first names. Others will even go as far as allocating each child in the class a French or German name in their first year of learning the language. Most children enjoy this, but some teachers feel there are drawbacks to a 'foreign' identity which outweigh the advantages. Another possibility is to use animal names or to devise your own foreign version of the Letterland characters. A selected list of common first names in French/German is included in Appendix 2. You will find fuller lists in the teacher's guides to some of the published courses.

There are some very attractive alphabet songs and chants in both French and German. Here are just three:

In **German** : Teacher solo: ABCDEFG   Children in Chorus echo: ABCDEFG
                           HLMNO-P   HLMNO-P
                           QRSTUVW   QRSTUVW
                           X Y Z   X Y Z

ABCD EFG HLMN O P QRST UVW X Y — Z

You can either use the melody printed here or get your children to compose their own.

In **French:**

	Chantons l'alphabet *
Teacher solo:	Chantons l'alphabet de A jusqu'à Z
	Pour le dire sans nous tromper
	La musique va nous aider
	ABCDEFG
	HIJKLMN
	OPQRSTU
	VWXYZ
	Allez-y, recommencez
	La musique va nous aider
Class joins in:	ABC, etc.
	Encore une fois s'il vous plaît
	Maintenant tout le monde sait
	ABC, etc.

L'étourdi **

A B C	qui a vu passer
D E F	la tête à Joseph
G H I	quand elle est partie
J K L	elle avait des ailes
M N O	pour aller là-haut
P Q R	voler dans les airs
S T U	n'est pas revenue
V W	pour la retrouver
X Y Z	il faut que tu m'aides.

*   *Ecoute et chante les lettres,* J et R Jeannot (Nathan)
** *Orange bleu,* Michel Beau (Nathan)
Both songs are recorded on cassette in *Le petit trampoline* (CLE).

EXTENSION

Higher up the school the children can be challenged to use the alphabet in speech and writing on a regular basis. They should be taught to ask:

Comment ça s'écrit? Vous pouvez épeler ça, s'il vous plaît?
Wie schreibt man das? Können Sie das buchstabieren, bitte?

and to write down new words from dictation as well as from the board.

A lot of fun can be derived from a telephone game where A rings up B in response to a party invitation. A has to spell out the full names of three more friends who would like to come to the party, i.e. pupil A dictates the names for B to write down:

A: *Allo. C'est toi Sylvie? Sylvie,*
    mes trois amis voudraient venir
    à la boum — tu es d'accord?
B: *Bon — d'accord. Comment s'appellent-ils?*
A: *Robert Boulanger, Gisèle Drieux et Anne Albert.*
B: *Tu peux épeler ça?*
A: *Oui. Alors . . . R O B E R T,* etc.

Likewise, a geographical information gap task could be created where each of the pair has an outline map of France/Germany with five place names plotted and five place names missing. A has to find out from B the missing towns numbered on his map and B does likewise. Both have to write in the town names from dictation:

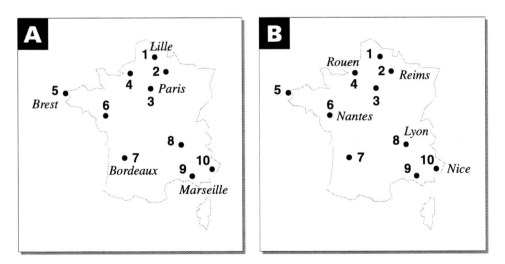

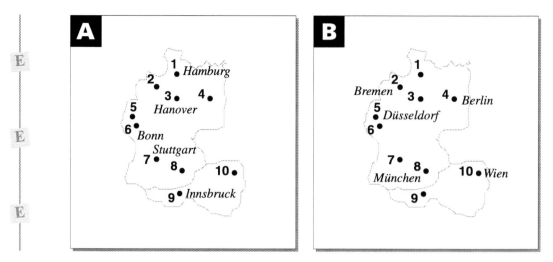

NUMBERS

BASIC

There are many counting rhymes in French and German, but it is important to find one that is matched to the needs of your class. A small selection is included here. You will find lots more in French/German children's books.

In German:

> Eins, zwei, Polizei
> Drei, vier, Offizier
> Fünf, sechs, alte Hex'
> Sieben, acht, gute Nacht!
> Neun, zehn, auf Wiederseh'n!

1, 2,
3, 4,
5, 6,
7, 8,
9, 10,

This rhyme can be practised initially with children counting on their fingers, but as the class gets into the ryhthm it is much more fun to have them walking round the room and inventing actions for each line, like those suggested in the visuals.

This well-known German '*Abzählreim*' is the equivalent to the English:
One potato, two potato, three potato, four . . . and may appeal to small children:

In French:

(This is really a playground game and should ideally be played outdoors; it calls for the children to make different kinds of steps as they say/sing each verse.)

PAS à PAS

1 pas		8 pas de charge	
2 pas		9 pas de loup	Je marche pas à pas
3 pas	Je marche pas à pas		
		Encore un pas	
4 grands pas		Ça fait 10 pas	Je marche pas à pas
5 grands pas	Je marche pas à pas		
		Mais pas 1 pas	
6 pas de course		Ça fait zéro	Et je ne marche pas.
7 pas de danse	Je marche pas à pas		

The traditional song below is a little more complicated to learn as it makes demands on pronunciation, but the tune is repeated for each of the first three lines with only a minor variation in the last line.

1 2 3 allons dans les bois.   4 5 6 cueillir des cerises.   7 8 9 dans mon

panier neuf.   10 11 12 elles seront toutes rouges.

If you are looking for a more lively way of practising the numbers in song, the '*Ballade des chiffres*' in *Le français en chantant* (Didier) is a really catchy number that invites children to put actions to the words:

1 2 3	claque tes doigts.	14 15	comme le singe.
4 5 6	tape tes cuisses.	16 17	sur ta tête.
Voilà 7	sur ta tête.	18 19 20	on recommence, frappe dans
8 et 9 et 10	tous les enfants applaudissent.		tes mains.
11 12 13	sur ta chaise.	1 2 3 4 5 6 7 8	il faut maintenant apprendre la suite.

There are lots of possible number games to provide more practice: loto, dominoes that match the number to the word, simple snap games in pairs where pupils count one or two numbers in turn:

A: *un*
B: *deux, trois*
A: *quatre, cinq*
B: *six . . .*   Whoever says 11 first is the winner (or 21, or 31).

You can also introduce simple addition and subtraction sums in the foreign language for fun at quite an early stage: children can write down the numbers simply from listening to the sums in French/German:

Un et deux? font: 3   *Sechs und zwei? macht : 8*

A simple way of extending the numbers to twenty could go like this:

10 + 1	onze
10 + 2	douze
10 + 3	treize . . . c'est pour Thérèse
10 + 4	quatorze
10 + 5	quinze
10 + 6	seize . . . et c'est pour Blaise
10 + 7	dix-sept
10 + 8	dix-huit
10 + 9	dix-neuf . . . alors, quoi de neuf?
10 + 10	vingt . . .

Vingt lapins pour Benjamin.

And you will find more rhymes and *comptines* in *1, 2, 3 compte avec moi* from Nathan.

There is of course plenty of scope for children to use dice or dominoes in pairs to practise saying the numbers aloud — and you can get them to make dominoes or spinners that go beyond six if you wish.

When the children are confident with a given range of numbers, you can play '*buzz*' with them as a whole class or group activity:

1, 2, 3, 4, . . . zut;   *1, 2, Pfui! . . . 4, 5,* etc.

If a child says the chosen number by mistake, he has to stand up.

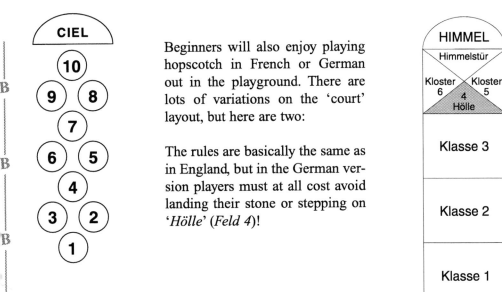

Beginners will also enjoy playing hopscotch in French or German out in the playground. There are lots of variations on the 'court' layout, but here are two:

The rules are basically the same as in England, but in the German version players must at all cost avoid landing their stone or stepping on 'Hölle' (Feld 4)!

EXTENSION

In the *Telephone Book* game the class can be divided into two teams: team A receives a list of the names of team B and vice versa. In turn each child asks someone in the opposite team:

> Team A: *Philippe, quel est ton numéro de téléphone?*
> Team B: Philippe replies: *Mon numéro est: 37 68 94*

All the children in team A have to write in the number by Philippe's name on the list. The team that has the most accurate list is the winner.

NB: At the early stages of number work the teacher will have to restrict the range of telephone numbers and the children will read them: *trois-sept-six-huit-neuf-quatre*. When they are older and more confident, they can practise the higher numbers up to 100 using the same game; this time they can be challenged to say the phone numbers in pairs as the French, Germans, Swiss and Austrians do:

> *trente-sept, soixante-huit, quatre-vingt-quatorze*
> *siebenunddreißig, achtundsechzig, vierundneunzig*

Many Scottish primary schools have found it rewarding to hold a quick oral mental arithmetic session at the beginning of a lesson, progressing from simple sums ($2 \times 9 - 3 = ?$ $12 + 7 = ?$) to more complex teasers:

> *vingt-huit plus quatre-vingt-treize moins onze =???*
> *zweiunddreißig weniger sechzehn mal zwei = ??*

THE CALENDAR
DAYS, MONTHS, SEASON, WEATHER

BASIC

As you gradually build the children's command of the numbers up to 31, you can begin to establish a daily calendar, preferably on a ready-made board with numbers, days, months and, if you wish, weather symbols which can be changed/added daily. This is infinitely more rewarding than just writing the date on a chalkboard.

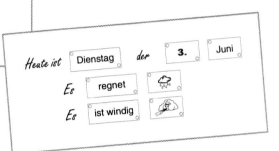

Aujourd'hui c'est le | lundi | **7** | mai

Il y a | du vent

Il fait | beau

NB: Be careful to teach the date correctly: the French do **not** say: *lundi le 7 mai* — as we do; in reply to your question: *Quel jour sommes-nous?* you should teach the children:
On est le jeudi 4 avril before introducing them to the long word *aujourd'hui*.
And the Germans/Austrians do not write *den* or *der* in front of the date any more:
3. Juni 1996 or: *3. 6. 1996* is what appears on letters, but you **do** need to teach the children the phrase: *Heute ist **der** 8. Mai* — in answer to the question: *Der wievielte ist heute?*

There are several useful rhymes and jingles to help the children memorise the days of the week and it is easy to make up your own simple tunes in class if you want to sing them. In French this well-known rhyme is a good standby:

Bonjour, Madame Lundi!
Comment va Madame Mardi?
Très bien, Madame Mercredi.
Dites à Madame Jeudi
De venir Vendredi
Danser Samedi
Dans la salle de Dimanche.

(recorded on the cassettes to *Trampoline 1*)

To teach the greetings at different times of the day you could get the children to make up their own little tune like this:

(class echo)

Bonjour! Bonjour! Bonsoir! Bonsoir! Bonne nuit! Bonne nuit! Au revoir! Au revoir!

Guten Morgen! Guten Tag! Guten Abend! Gute Nacht!

To attach the times of day to mealtimes you might create a simple rap based on this rhythm:

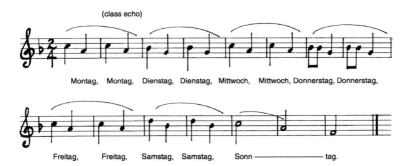

Le matin on prend le petit déjeuner,
A midi on prend le déjeuner.
L'après-midi on prend le goûter
Et le soir on mange le dîner.

The days of the week can be practised in many different contexts, but one of the simplest techniques is to sing them; the tune below relies on the principle of the children echoing the teacher in a very simple way:

(class echo)

Montag, Montag, Dienstag, Dienstag, Mittwoch, Mittwoch, Donnerstag, Donnerstag,

Freitag, Freitag, Samstag, Samstag, Sonn ———— tag.

It is quite a simple matter to make up a variation on this tune with a shape and rhythm to match the different intonation required for French.

EXTENSION

For older children there is an attractive little song: 'Combien de jours' on a useful cassette from Canada by Matt (Muffin Record Co) (ESB):

Combien de jours dans la semaine?	Lundi, mardi, mercredi, jeudi, } BIS
Dites-moi, est-ce que vous savez?	Vendredi, samedi, dimanche. }
Combien de jours dans la semaine?	
Il y en a sept, je vous assure, c'est vrai.	Verses 2 and 3 cover the months and the seasons.

A further development of the weather/seasons theme could be the drawing of a large map of France/Germany on which the children plot the previous day's **real** temperatures and weather from reports in the daily newspapers. These are presumably already available on the Internet!

If the school has its own weather station equipment, the class could keep its own log in the target language of local weather. This would practise a number of skills — scientific observation and measurement, accurate record keeping, maths and language combined.

LE TEMPS

Date:	6.7.96
Heure:	9h30
Température:	21°C
Vent du:	nord-ouest
Temps:	soleil / chaud

DAS WETTER HEUTE

Datum:	7.6.96
Uhrzeit:	9.30
Temperatur:	21°C
Wind aus:	Nordwesten
Wetter:	sonnig / warm

COLOURS

In a similar vein you can introduce beginners to the colours using a rainbow which restricts the repertoire to six or seven basic colours:

rouge/orange/jaune/vert/bleu/violet — rot/orange/gelb/grün/blau/violett

These can be combined with simple shape activities involving:

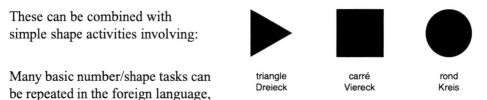

triangle	carré	rond
Dreieck	Viereck	Kreis

Many basic number/shape tasks can be repeated in the foreign language, helping to consolidate concepts and ideas from maths lessons.

Older juniors can progressively add other aspects of colour:

	bleu clair, vert foncé . . .	*hellblau, dunkelgrün . . .*
and add	*rose, brun, gris, noir, blanc, beige . . .*	*rosa, braun, grau, schwarz, weiß, beige . . .* as required.

Descriptions of people and clothes inevitably require more complicated structures and juniors will have to learn at some stage about the position of adjectives in French and the inflection of adjectives in German:

CILT

J'ai un petit chien brun et blanc . . .
Ich habe einen kleinen, braunweißen Hund.
Jane porte une jupe verte et un pull rouge.
Ian hat heute einen grauen Pullover und eine schwarze Hose an.

CLOTHES/WEATHER/HOLIDAYS

Infants classes can be introduced to the names of clothing we wear in winter to keep warm, such as: *Mantel, Schal, Handschuhe, Wollmütze/manteau, écharpe, gants, bonnet* and in summer to keep cool: *T-shirt, Short, Badehose, Bikini/T-shirt, short, maillot de bain,* using the suitcase game:

En janvier nous allons à X,	*Wir fahren im Januar nach X,*
en août nous allons à Y.	*im August nach Z.*
Qu'est-ce que tu mets dans ta valise?	*Was nimmst du mit?*
Je prends un pull, des gants, . . .	*Ich brauche einen Pullover, Handschuhe, . . .*

The juniors will need to progress to adding colours, sizes, too big/small and to clothes for different activities and occasions and all kinds of weather.

ANIMALS

The youngest children will be able to learn the names of pets, soft animals and certainly a few wild animals too, especially the easy cognates:

Eléphant/Elefant, Tigre/Tiger, Lion/Löwe, Girafe/Giraffe . . .

With the juniors you will be able to extend the repertoire much further to include the food the animals eat, the age and size of pets, the habitat and country of origin of wild animals and birds. The scope for reading and writing, if you can get hold of French/German children's books, is considerable and will depend on your own interests and enthusiasm.

BIRTHDAYS/CELEBRATIONS

With the youngest children it will be quite sufficient to celebrate individual birthdays with a rendering of:

Joyeux anniversaire, joyeux anniversaire,
joyeux anniversaire, Nicole, joyeux anniversaire

Zum Geburtstag viel Glück, zum Geburtstag viel Glück,
Viel Glück liebe(r) . . . , zum Geburtstag viel Glück.

to the tune of *Happy birthday* in both languages and perhaps count aloud and blow out the candles on a simple cake.

As the children get older it will be possible to extend the ceremonies to birthday games, to singing other songs, to making greeting cards and to involving the class in activities associated with namedays, Easter eggs, Christmas/New Year customs.

SCHOOL/CLASSROOM

Infants will need to be familar with only the basic classroom objects that they use daily as suggested in Chapter 3, but older pupils can be presented with more challenging tasks to include their school subjects, a plan of the school with rooms and facilities labelled and possibly a simple description of the school and its environment — a possible subject for a home-made video to send to a partner school abroad.

CILT

3   Displaying the target language

No primary teacher needs to be reminded of the value of classroom display: it is part of every teacher's stock in trade. There are many ways of weaving foreign language texts into the normal topics displayed in the classroom; your only major limitation will be space!

What we are talking about of course is not just a few tourist posters from France/Germany but a whole battery of items which link with the topic we are teaching and which will assist the **linguistic progress** and, at the same time, enhance the **cultural awareness** of the class.

If you are short of wall space to display your visuals, you can always adopt the well-tried trick of stringing two or three metres of washing line across a corner of the room and pegging your flashcards, realia, etc to the line — and there is always the ceiling!

The style of display and the artwork will depend very much on your own preferences and skills, but you will always have the talents of the children to call on and we hope the simple ideas in this chapter will spark off even better projects for your own classroom.

Starting with complete beginners, we can easily reinforce our bank of daily classroom instructions with visuals. It is relatively simple, for example, to produce flashcards or large mobiles to act as a prompt for the children, as suggested in Chapter 2 pp11–13.

THE ALPHABET

This can be presented and practised in a variety of ways; you might consider a classroom frieze gradually made, a few letters a week, by the children. The letters could be done in a variation on Letterland style, or they could be related to animals, food, or any other theme that seems appropriate — but make sure you have a good picture dictionary (e.g. Usborne) to help you!

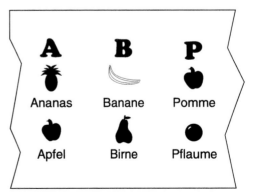

Alternatively, you could encourage the children to collect new words they discover each week in a pictionary box, as suggested in Chapter 2.

There are some further useful suggestions in the *Cahier d'activités* in *Trampoline 1*. Starting a pictionary box quite early on can help children relate the foreign word to the picture by handling it and sorting it into alphabetical order and by colour code to its gender.

NUMBERS

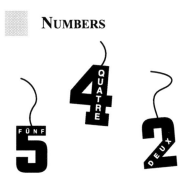

It is probably wise to teach the numbers initially in small doses (1–5, 6–10, 11–15 and so on), and it is obviously helpful to use every practical aid from the maths cupboard you can lay hands on. You could also hang numbers (made and painted by the children) as mobiles from the ceiling . . .

. . . or put them on double-sided domino cards:

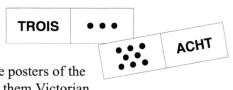

If your class is ready for it, you could even make posters of the 2x, 3x, 4x, 5x tables and get the class to recite them, Victorian style, in the target language:

> *Deux fois un font deux, deux fois deux font quatre, etc.*
> *Zweimal eins ist zwei, zweimal zwei ist vier, usw.*

There are numerous counting rhymes/songs in all languages (see the examples in Chapter 2).

Once your class can count to 31, you can relate the numbers to the months of the year. A calendar board is a really rewarding piece of equipment and, once made, saves a lot of time. A superb, but expensive, metal Calendar Board is produced by Nathan (see ESB catalogue), providing a variety of features, including the possibility of highlighting children's birthdays, but a DIY board can be created out of hardboard, plywood or MDF and painted along the lines of the illustrations on pp44 and 46.

BIRTHDAYS/NAMEDAYS

Once the class has begun to celebrate individual birthdays, a card or poster to hang on the wall might come in useful:

REALIA — A 'FOREIGN' CORNER

Whatever the age of your class there are numerous possibilities for making a French or German Corner in your classroom to create some 'ambience' of the foreign country. Here you could display realia — food packets, drinks, household gadgets, stamps, picture books, toys, games, tickets, photographs, brochures, maps — anything that will arouse children's natural curiosity about the countries where the language is spoken. It is a good idea to arrange this display **thematically** if you can, so that items brought out of the cupboard relate directly to the current topic.

You can go further than this if you like by getting the class to help you create a French/German model village or even a shop with a counter which can remain in situ for a whole term (if you have the room!). This then becomes the focus for role play and improvised shopping scenes, replacing fruit and vegetables with ice creams, clothes, shoes, sweets, as appropriate. Imitation coins and banknotes are available from French/German publishers (see Resources list).

PHRASES OF THE WEEK

Whatever stage your class has reached, you may find it helps the children to memorise key phrases for classroom interaction if you display on the wall near the board three or four 'Phrases of the week'. If you have just taught them to ask for permission to do something, the list might look like this:

Excusez-moi, madame . . .	Entschuldigen Sie, Frau X . . .
Je peux . . .	Darf ich bitte . . .
sortir,	hinausgehen?
aller aux toilettes,	auf die Toilette gehen?
aller chercher mon stylo, s'il vous plaît?	meinen Kugelschreiber holen?

Classroom equipment

In the classroom you can help them to memorise everyday objects and equipment by ensuring that they are permanently labelled in French or German and colour-coded for gender:

le placard	la table
le bureau	la porte
le tiroir	la fenêtre
le tableau	la télévision
le magnétophone	la poubelle
l'ordinateur	la lumière
le rétroprojecteur	

der Tisch	die Tür	das Pult
der Schrank	die Schublade	das Licht
der Abfalleimer	die Tafel	das Fenster
der Fernseher		
der Computer		

The children's contribution

To help the teacher from time to time, the children can be encouraged to contribute to the classroom display themselves. They can make very good flashcards (often clearer and more colourful than commercially produced ones) and these can be laminated for durability and constant handling. If you are using a set of published teaching materials, the children would enjoy making large versions of the cartoon characters who appear in the books. They will also get a lot of enjoyment out of creating collages, making displays of their own pets, adding a simple description and a drawing or photograph, e.g.:

Voici mon chaton.
Il s'appelle Perky.
Il a six mois.
Il est noir et blanc et jaune.

They could do the same
with wild animals:

J'aime les phoques.
Les phoques habitent au Canada.
Voici un bébé-phoque. Il est blanc.

Older juniors will enjoy creating their own monsters
which they can draw and paint or make models of:

Voilà un ELELOUP
Il a trois jambes et un long museau.
Il est noir, jaune et rouge.
Il mange les champignons et les pommes frites.

 BRICOLAGE/BASTELN

Many primary schools combine manual skills with language learning by encouraging
the children to design and make models based on their own experiences abroad or on
video material that has been shown in class. For example, a class could make a fantasy
or 'real' French/German village or a market place, including cobbled streets, market
stalls and shops of various kinds:

boucherie, boulangerie/pâtisserie, journaux/papeterie, tabac, poste
Metzgerei, Bäckerei, Tabakwaren, Postamt, Obst und Gemüse, . . .

SIGNPOSTS

If you wish to make more of an impact on the whole school by showing every parent and
visitor that a foreign language really is taught here, then you can enlist the children's cre-
ativity by inviting them to design and make your own signposts for the school entrance
and corridors. It is bound to make an immediate and positive impression on
visitors, e.g:

The children may well think of lots of other parts of the school that need a signpost or labelling of some kind.

You need not restrict your foreign language labelling to these items, however. You may well find opportunities to weave the foreign language into other areas of the curriculum. If you have a classroom display relating to maths, geography, science or history, it may be possible to add some simple labels in French or German. Collages of clothes, leaves, trees, wildlife, dinosaurs, space travel, for example, can be labelled bilingually, if you think it appropriate. The labelling need only be one word captions for younger classes, but children in the juniors should be encouraged to read longer sentences or short descriptive paragraphs.

CHILDREN'S WRITING

It is important to young language learners that their artwork and their first attempts at writing should be valued by the teacher and displayed in the classroom as often as possible. The range is considerable, from simple personal profiles, like the *Carte d'identité/Personalausweis* (see p36) to family trees: these can be devised in humorous ways, using a ficticious family as a starting point, but with the ultimate aim of enabling each child to draw his or her own real family tree and talk about it in the target language.

The children can of course find photographs or simply make drawings of their family. You may find this a good opportunity to include word-processing skills for the captions if the display is to be created over several weeks.

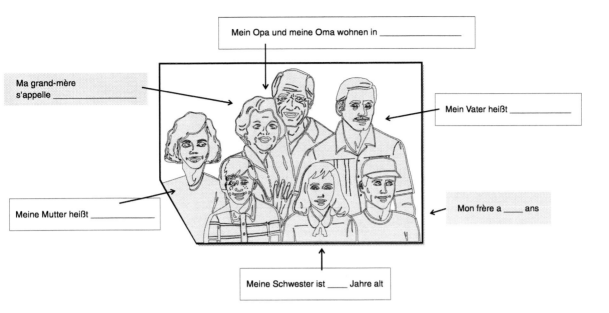

Mein Opa und meine Oma wohnen in _____

Ma grand-mère s'appelle _____

Mein Vater heißt _____

Meine Mutter heißt _____

Mon frère a ____ ans

Meine Schwester ist ____ Jahre alt

MY HOME

If you teach the topic of homes and the rooms in a house/flat, the children may enjoy making a sketch of their own home, based on a model you have provided. This can include measurements on a ground plan if you think they can benefit from using their mathematical skills as well. (See also further activities in *Superspiele/Jeux faciles* which would lend themselves to display.)

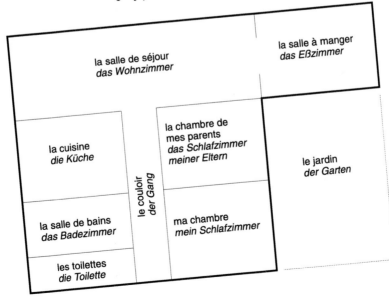

la salle de séjour
das Wohnzimmer

la salle à manger
das Eßzimmer

la cuisine
die Küche

la chambre de mes parents
das Schlafzimmer meiner Eltern

le jardin
der Garten

le couloir
der Gang

la salle de bains
das Badezimmer

ma chambre
mein Schlafzimmer

les toilettes
die Toilette

SURVEYS AND GRAPHS

Mathematical skills can also be practised in the foreign language through class surveys of various kinds. The children can collect data on their classmates' pets, favourite foods, drinks, ice creams, sports, or the places they have visited on holiday. A survey provides an opportunity for lots of speaking/listening practice combined with the need to record answers and then present the results in some form of graph. By the end of the lesson even the slowest child should have asked and heard the question:

Qu'est-ce que tu préfères comme glace?/Welche Eissorte ißt du am liebsten?
OR: *Tu as un animal?/Hast du ein Haustier?*
OR: *Qu'est-ce que tu aimes comme sport?/Welchen Sport treibst du gern?*

at least 25 times! The final results can be displayed as a pie-chart/blockgraph with appropriate colour coding:

Nous aimons bien les glaces.
Nous préférons:
Wir essen gern Eis.
Unsere Lieblingssorten sind:

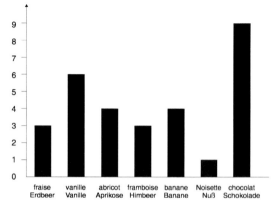

LINKS WITH PARTNER SCHOOLS ABROAD

If your school has no foreign links as yet, a short-term substitute could be a pupil correspondence with another class in a nearby school, provided that you and the class teacher have agreed the 'rules of the game' and that the target language is used throughout. This is no long-term solution, but it does create a genuine 'information gap' and allows the children to use the target language for a real purpose. Links with a primary school abroad can lead to some of the most motivating events for the children. The arrival of a new batch of letters or a large parcel from the partner school is bound to cause excitement. The display of a selection of the letters and photographs creates a buzz throughout the class and attracts curiosity from the rest of the school. You can get help in setting up links with a partner school abroad from the Schools Unit of the Central Bureau (CBEVE) (see Appendix 4). While it may seem premature to many teachers to attempt such a link with very young children, there are a few infant schools where children as young as six and seven have successfully spent a week in France, on reciprocal visits. It is certainly an enormous bonus and eye-opener for children of eight or nine to start a correspondence with a primary class abroad and, if it can be arranged, to have their first taste of the foreign culture on a week's visit to the country, visiting a primary school in the process and meeting their penfriends. There are many such partnerships which have led to much wider exchanges of materials and information covering the whole curriculum and involving the whole of the staff.

In many primary schools impressive work is displayed by junior children resulting from a week's residential visit to France where they have been given a variety of cross-curricular tasks, including studies and drawings of the built environment, transects of a small village, town trails and historical studies. The possibilities of geographical/historical studies are endless, provided that the teachers know the area well and that the pupils have been well prepared beforehand. More than one school, for example, has taken children to Monet's garden, encouraging them to sit and paint in his style.

IT AND CD-ROM

Much use can be made of computers to enhance the scope of your display if your school can afford to invest in some simple word-processing packages, such as *European Folio, Fun with texts, Pendown, Storybook Weaver* (CD-ROM). Children of all abilities can be helped to write simple descriptions of their home, their pets, their family. These can be complemented by drawings or photos as appropriate. As they progress in the juniors they can be encouraged to recombine the phrases they have learnt to create a simple first letter to a penfriend like the one on p58.

BOOKMAKING/CLASS NEWSPAPERS

As pupils progress through the junior school it will be increasingly possible for them to create stories, make cartoon-strip books or short playlets of their own. Here again the computer could be used to assist in drafting and redrafting a script or book text.

The idea of a monthly newsletter/newspaper may appeal to some classes. This could be word-processed or desktop published in the form of one or two sides of A4 posted on the wall every few weeks. After initial guidance from you, the newspaper could become the responsibility of a small 'editorial committee' of children who gather together contributions from the class: puzzles, poems, quizzes, news of recent/forthcoming school events, items about individual pupils (or teachers!), jokes — or just plain gossip!

It is amazing what children can create with a very limited range of grammar and vocabulary once their enthusiasm is fired.

Notre courrier

EXTRA!

Anne et Katy en France

Portrait
d'un prof

Nous gagnons
au foot! 4 à 1

Animal perdu

Unsere Zeitung

EXTRA!

Barry und Trevor in Berlin

Ein
Gedicht

Tim hat
gewonnen!

Unser Puzzle

Croydon, le 3 mai 1995

Chère amie

Je m'appelle Samantha.
Comment t'appelles-tu?
J'habite à Selsdon.
Où habites-tu?
J'ai dix ans.
Et toi, quel âge as-tu?
Mon anniversaire, c'est en
avril.
Quelle est la date de ton
anniversaire?

amitiés,

Samantha

Conclusion

Getting Started

Using the list of target language phrases in Appendix 1 as your starting point, select a small number of phrases you are going to concentrate on each week, and try to build up your repertoire slowly, making sure the children get used to a core of your instructions/comments. After a few weeks you can gradually progress to new phrases and situations, but it is advisable to script your target language quite clearly in lesson plans or you will forget to include some phrases or neglect to revise them regularly.

Once you are confident that your target language is secure and that the children understand you, it is time to consider scripting and teaching the language that you want **them** to use actively in games, role play and repartee with each other. In teaching this language for class interaction you will find a lot of help in the pack *Cartoons for classroom communication* published by Miniflashcards (1996). The language the children will need for games and role play will depend very much on the topics you select, but here you will find help in YPF2. If, through your LEA, you can gain access to the substantial resources from the SOED, you will find inspiration in the three videos *MLs in the primary school* and in the training materials for French and German (same title).

Finding in-service support

If you teach in Scotland or one of the Southern English LEAs, you may be able to attend locally run in-service training courses designed specifically for primary/special school teachers. Your first point of enquiry should be your LEA languages adviser/advisory teacher.

CILT runs regular in-house workshops in London and also occasional one-day, two-day or residential conferences in other parts of the country, e.g. in Manchester. CILT also offers courses for teachers of young learners in Germany (in collaboration with the Goethe-Institut) and in Spain (in collaboration with the Spanish Embassy and the Government of Navarra). These involve linguistic and methodological updating.

FURTHER PROFESSIONAL DEVELOPMENT

You could start your own professional development by working your way through the Bibliography in Appendix 3, concentrating particularly on the primary specific items marked (p). You could also extend your repertoire and confidence in teaching in the target language by:

- familiarising yourself with the authentic teaching materials published in France/Germany (see ESB catalogue and the European Bookshop) where you will find much of the language you need to teach familiar topics;

- calling on the help of a native speaker parent and, if you can, using him or her as an informal classroom assistant and language consultant;

- begging, borrowing, stealing a Foreign Language Assistant (FLA) from your local secondary school or LEA for a short period in the summer term (NB: Richmond, Croydon and Manchester now recruit FLAs to work specifically in their primary schools for the whole year through LINGUA funding);

- investing, if possible, in video materials such as *Pilote* and *3, 2, 1 . . . Los!* as a core visual resource round which to build work for one or even two years. The teachers' notes to these courses are particularly helpful to non-specialist teachers and include 'Classroom language' sections to help you with target language phrases;

- trying to make contact with a French/Belgian/Swiss, German/Austrian/Swiss primary school. This will motivate both you and your children to broaden the range of classroom activities and bring almost overnight a breath of up-to-date, authentic foreign language and culture into your school;

- borrowing and plagiarising ideas and materials from native speakers, secondary language teachers, adult education tutors, your own colleagues in school — they all have a secret repertoire of games and activities that you can easily adapt to suit the age and interests of your class.

CILT

Appendix 1 Target language for classroom interaction

In a book of this size it is not possible to provide a fully comprehensive list of phrases you may need one day in class. but we have attempted to offer a basic list as a starting point for non-specialist teachers covering most of the situations outlined on p10.

Note: Linguistic and/or cultural items that need special attention from the teacher are highlighted with a [g] for grammar or [c] for culture.

1 Arriving at the classroom

Rangez-vous!	Get in line, please.	Eine Reihe, bitte!
Vite, mettez-vous en rangs!	Line up quickly!	Schön einreihen!
On se met en rangs!	Queue up properly!	Stellt euch schön an!
		Schlange stehen, bitte!
Simon, range-toi!	Simon, get in line!	Simon, stell dich brav an!
Stéphanie, tu te ranges, stp.		
Taisez-vous!	Quiet, please!	Ruhe, bitte!
Vous vous taisez, svp.		Seid jetzt still, bitte!
Alain, tais-toi!	Alan, be quiet!	Alan, sei still!
Tu me laisses passer?	Can I come past?	Darf ich bitte vorbei?
Laissez-moi passer!	Let me through, please!	Laßt mich bitte vorbei!
Vous me laisser passer, messieurs!	Let me come past.	Ich möchte vorbei, meine Herren!
Entrez!	In you go!	Geht hinein!
Allez-y!	Go in!	Los!
On y va!		Auf geht's!
En silence, svp!	In silence, please!	In Ruhe, bitte!
Avancez en silence!		Geht leise hinein!

[g] *Vous* for the whole class/several pupils; *Tu* for individuals.
The phrases: '*s'il te plaît*' and '*s'il vous plaît*' have been abbreviated to 'stp' and 'svp' throughout these lists.

2 Greetings

Bonjour!	Good morning!	Guten Morgen!
Bonjour, tout le monde!		Guten Tag! Grüß Gott!*
Ça va?	How are you all?	Wie geht's (euch)?
Ça va mieux, Julie?	Are you better, Julia?	Geht's dir jetzt besser, Julia?
Bon, asseyez-vous!	Good. Sit down please.	Gut. Setzt euch, bitte!
Assieds-toi vite, Ben!	Quickly, Ben — sit down!	Ben, setz dich schnell, bitte!

[c] French teachers do **not** say: '*Bonjour la classe*' or '*Bonjour les enfants!*'
These are anglicisms that should be avoided.
'*Salut!*' is a familiar greeting amongst friends: P/P but **not** T/P or P/T.

[c] * '*Guten Tag!*' and '*Grüß Gott!*' can be used at any time of day until the evening, when you say
'*Guten Abend!*' '*Grüß Gott!*' is the normal greeting in Bavaria and Austria, but is not used in North
Germany.
'*Hallo!*' is a common informal greeting among children and young people.

3   Getting settled

Qui ferme la porte?	Who is shutting the door?	Wer macht die Tür zu?
Bernard, tu fermes la porte, stp!	Bernard, shut the door please.	Bernd, mach die Tür zu, bitte!
Paul, mets la balle sous la table.	Paul, put the ball under the table.	Paul, leg den Ball unter den Tisch!
Tu poses la balle dans le placard/ dans le coin.	Put the ball in the cupboard/ in the corner.	Du legst bitte den Ball in den Schrank/in die Ecke.
Claire et Sylvie, arrêtez de bavarder!	C and S stop chattering!	Clare und Sylvia, hört jetzt auf zu plaudern.
Taisez-vous, maintenant!	Be quiet now!	Seid endlich einmal still!
Bon, taisez-vous!		Seid still, bitte!
Stéphane, un peu de calme, svp!	S, let's have some quiet.	Stefan, du sollst still sein, ja?
Ecoutez!	Listen!	Hört zu!
Attention, svp!	Pay attention.	Paßt gut auf!

4   Calling the register

Alors, tout le monde est là?	Is everyone here?	Also, seid ihr alle da?
Bon, je fais l'appel.	I'm calling the register.	Wer hat das Klassenbuch, bitte?*
On va faire/commence par l'appel.		Gut. Ich rufe jetzt die Namen auf.
Où sont Sandrine et Laura?	Where are S and L?	Wo sind Sabine und Lore?
S. et L, où sont-elles?		Sind S und L noch nicht da?
Laura n'est pas là?	Is L not here?	Lore ist nicht da?
Où est-elle?	Where is she then?	Wo ist sie denn?
Stéphane est absent?	Is S away?	Stefan fehlt?
Il est malade?	Is he ill?	Ist er krank?
Qui mange à la cantine aujourd'hui?	Who is having a school dinner today?	Wer ißt heute zu Mittag in der Kantine?
Levez la main, si vous mangez/ ceux qui mangent à la cantine aujourd'hui.	Put up your hand if you are having a school meal today.	Hebt die Hand, wenn ihr heute in der Kantine eßt.
Qui déjeune à la cantine à midi?	Who is having a school dinner today?	Wer bleibt zum Mittagessen in der Schule?**

Ci**LT**

[c] * The *Klassenbuch* in Germany/Austria is not just an attendance register; it is also a record of grades (1–6) awarded to pupils by subject teachers and is usually taken by a pupil from lesson to lesson for the teacher to sign.

** School dinners are virtually unknown in most parts of Germany/Austria; most children go home to lunch between 1 and 2 o'clock — the end of the school day.

5 Organising ourselves

Pierre, assieds-toi!	P sit down.	Peter, setz dich!
Assieds-toi, stp Sylvain!	R/S sit down please.	Setz dich bitte Reinhard!
Je t'attends, dépêche-toi!	Hurry up, I'm waiting.	Mach schnell. Ich warte!
On vous attend, dépêchez-vous!	Quick, we're all waiting.	Schnell! Wir warten auf euch.
Alain, tu poses ton cartable, stp!	A put your bag down.	Alan, stell die Tasche hin, bitte!
Posez votre cartable par terre, svp.	Put all your bags on the floor.	Stellt eure Taschen hin!
Anne, tu enlèves ton manteau/ ton anorak, stp!	A take your coat/anorak off.	Anna, zieh deinen Mantel/ deinen Anorak aus!
Tout le monde est assis?	Sit down everyone.	Setzt euch jetzt!
Ça y est?	Are we ready?	Sind wir soweit?
Bon, on va commencer.	Let's begin.	Gut. Wir fangen an/wir beginnen.
Sortez vite votre cahier/trousse votre trousse/votre stylo/ vos crayons.	You need your exercise books pencil case/a biro/your pencils.	Ihr braucht euer Heft/eure Federtasche/einen Kugel- schreiber/eure Farbstifte.
Denis, tu as ta trousse?	D have you got your pencil case?	Dieter, hast du deine Federtasche?
Tu n'a pas de stylo?	Haven't you got a biro?	Hast du keinen Kugelschreiber?

6 Getting attention

Bon. Taisez-vous maintenant!	Quiet now, please.	Also, Ruhe jetzt!
Paul, tais-toi donc!	P, stop talking,	Paul, sei doch still!
Je vous attends!	I'm waiting.	Ich warte auf dich/euch!
On t'attend, Philippe!	P we're all waiting for you.	Philip, wir warten alle auf dich!
Taisez-vous les autres!	The rest of you be quiet!	Hallo! Still sein, bitte!
Ça suffit!	That's enough now!	Das genügt!/ Jetzt hab' ich genug!
C'est fini! C'est terminé!	Stop it!	Schluß damit! Hört jetzt auf!

7 Setting the programme for the lesson

Bon. Aujourd'hui on va . . .	Today we are going to . . .	Also, heute werden wir . . .
écouter la cassette.	listen to the cassette.	uns die Kassette anhören.
regarder une vidéo.	watch a video.	uns einen Video ansehen.
regarder la télé.	watch television.	fernsehen.
répéter les numéros 11 à 20.	revise the numbers 11–20.	die Nummern von 11–20 wiederholen.

chanter une chanson.	sing a song.	ein Lied singen.
apprendre un poème/ une comptine.	learn a new poem/song.	ein neues Gedicht/ein neues Lied lernen.
réviser les . . .	revise the . . .	die . . . wiederholen
Tout d'abord on va . . .	First we are going to . . .	Zuerst einmal wollen wir . . .
Ensuite vous allez lire/ écrire/dessiner . . .	Then you will read/ write/draw . . .	Dann werdet ihr lesen/ schreiben/zeichnen . . .
Et enfin nous allons chanter/ jouer à un jeu.	And at the end we'll sing/ play a game.	Und zum Schluß wollen wir singen/ein Spiel machen.

8   Starting the lesson

Bon alors, vous sortez votre trousse/votre cahier de brouillon.	Now you will need your pencil case/your rough book.	Gut. Ihr braucht eure Feder- tasche/euer Notizheft.
Vous prenez une feuille de brouillon/papier.	Take a sheet of paper.	Ihr nehmt ein Blatt Papier.
Vous aurez besoin de votre classeur; des ciseaux; d'un stylo feutre comme ça.	You need your folder; scissors; a felt-tip like this.	Ihr braucht eure Mappe; eine Schere; so einen Filzstift.
Brian, tu vas chercher les feuilles de papier, stp.	B, you fetch the paper, please.	B, du holst uns das Papier, bitte.
Anne, tu vas chercher les ciseaux, stp.	A can you bring the scissors, please?	Anne, du bringst die Scheren, ja?
Richard, tu donnes les cahiers/les livres, stp.	R you give out the exercise books.	R, du teilst bitte die Hefte aus.
Vous avez tout ce qu'il vous faut?	Have you got everything?	Habt ihr jetzt alles?
Bon. On va commencer.	Good. Let's begin.	Na gut. Also fangen wir an.
On commence par l'exercice 2 à la page 7.	We'll start with exercise 2 on page 7.	Wir beginnen mit Aufgabe 2 auf Seite 7.
Je vais vous montrer ce qu'on va faire.	I'll show you how to do it.	Ich zeige euch, wie das geht.
Regardez et écoutez bien!	Watch and listen carefully.	Schaut her und hört gut zu!

9   Are you sitting comfortably?

Vous voyez tous le tableau/ l'écran?	Can you all see the board/ screen?	Könnt ihr alle die Tafel/ die Leinwand gut sehen?
Philippe, viens t'asseoir à côté de Roger.	P, come and sit next to R.	P, komm setz dich neben Roger.
Qui ne voit pas bien?	Who still can't see?	Wer kann nicht gut sehen?
Alors, prends ta chaise et viens ici.	Bring your chair and come here.	Also, nimm deinen Stuhl und komm her!

10   Discussing the date/weather

Quel date sommes-nous aujourd'hui?	What is the date today?	Der wievielte ist heute?
C'est mercredi?	Is it Wednesday?	Ist heute Mittwoch?
Quel mois sommes-nous?	Which month is it?	Welcher Monat ist es?
Qui peut nous dire/écrire la date?	Who can tell us/write the date for us?	Wer kann uns das Datum sagen/schreiben?
Et quel temps fait-il?	What is the weather like?	Und wie ist das Wetter heute?
Qui va changer/chercher l'image sur notre plan?	Who is going to change the weather symbol on our chart/ weather house?	Wer wechselt das Wetterbild auf unserer Wetterkarte/in unserem Wetterhäuschen?
Qui sait la température aujourd'hui?	Who can tell us the temperature?	Wer kann uns die Temperatur sagen?
Lève la main si c'est ton anniversaire/ta fête aujourd'hui.	Put up your hand is it's your birthday/nameday today.	Heb die Hand, wenn du heute Geburtstag/Namenstag hast.

11   Recapping

Hier/lundi/la semaine dernière . . .	Yesterday/on Monday/ last week . . .	Gestern/am Montag/letzte Woche . . .
nous avons chanté . . .	we sang	haben wir . . . gesungen
récité . . ./appris . . .	recited . . ./learnt . . .	. . . aufgesagt/. . . gelernt
joué à . . ./dit . . .	played . . ./said . . .	. . . gespielt/. . . gesagt

12   Presenting a new topic

Aujourd'hui /maintenant nous allons/on va . . .	Today/now we are going to . . .	Heute/jetzt wollen wir . . .
Ecoutez bien!	Listen carefully!	Paßt gut auf! Hört zu!
On va écouter la cassette/ regarder la vidéo/lire le poème à haute voix.	We'll listen to the cassette/ watch the video/ read the poem aloud.	Wir hören uns die Kassette an/ schauen uns den Video an/ lesen zusammen das Gedicht.

13   Setting up an activity

Vous allez travailler à 2/à 3/ en petits groupes de 4/5.	Work in two/threes/ groups of 4/5.	Ihr arbeitet zu zweit/zu dritt/ in Gruppen von 4/5.
Vous allez vous mettre par 3/par 4.	Get into groups of 3/4.	Bildet Gruppen zu dritt/zu viert.
Vous pouvez choisir votre partenaire.	Choose a partner.	Ihr könnt einen Partner wählen.
On va faire deux équipes: A et B.	We'll have two teams: Team A and Team B.	Wir machen zwei Mannschaften: Team A und Team B.
Vous travaillez tous seuls.	Work on your own today.	Ihr arbeitet heute allein.

14 Explaining

Vous avez compris?/ vous comprenez?	Has everyone understood?	Habt ihr verstanden? Alles OK?
Qui n'a pas compris?	Who doesn't understand?	Wer hat nicht verstanden?
Lève le doigt si tu n'as pas compris.	Put your hand up if you don't understand.	Melde dich, wenn du nicht verstehst.
Philippe, tu as compris, hein?	P, do you follow?	Philip, du hast verstanden, ja?
Pas de problèmes?	No problems?	Kein Problem?
Carole, tu peux nous expliquer en anglais?/nous montrer ce qu'on va faire?	C, can you explain that in English?/show us how you do it?	C, kannst du uns das auf Englisch erklären?/uns zeigen, wie man das macht?
Bon, ça y est?	Good. That's it!	Gut. So geht's, ja?
Allez-y! Au travail!	Right. You can start.	Fangt an. Los geht's!
On commence. Dépêchez-vous!	Come on — hurry up!	Ihr könnt schon beginnen. Macht schnell!

15 Monitoring progress

Paul, c'est bien ça. Ça c'est beau/c'est joli.	That's good, P, very nice.	Das ist gut, Petra. Ja, das ist sehr schön.
C'est très bien! Excellent!	Excellent! Super!	Prima! Ausgezeichnet!
Le dessin est très beau./ J'aime bien ton dessin!	That's a lovely picture. I like that very much.	Das Bild ist sehr schön. Deine Zeichnung gefällt mir gut!
Super! Bravo! Mes félicitations!	Bravo! Congratulations!	Super! Bravo! Ich gratuliere!
Ça c'est beaucoup mieux.	That's much better.	Das ist viel besser.
Regardez tout le monde!	Look everyone. That's really great, isn't it?	Schaut alle her! Das ist wirklich toll, nicht wahr?
C'est super, non?		
J et M, au travail!	J and M, get down to work.	J und M, ihr seid heute faul!
Il faut vous concentrer.	Pay attention/concentrate.	Paßt doch auf!
R, ça suffit maintenant! C'est fini!	R, that's enough of that!	R, das ist jetzt genug! Hör auf!
F, stp! Tais-toi!	F, please be quiet!	F, jetzt bist du endlich still!
X, tu n'a pas écouté ce qu'on a dit!	X you didn't listen!	X, du hast nicht aufgepaßt!

16 Explaining the rules of a game

Je vais vous expliquer comment jouer à ce jeu.	I'll show you how to play this game.	Ich sage euch, wie das geht.
Voici ce qu'on va faire.	This is how it goes . . .	So geht das . . .
Ecoutez bien!	Listen carefully!	Paßt gut auf!
La personne A commence . . .	A begins . . .	A beginnt . . .
Il/Elle pose la question.	He/She asks a question.	Er/Sie stellt eine Frage.
Il/Elle jette le dé.	He/She throws the dice.	Er/Sie würfelt.
Il/Elle décrit l'image.	He/She describes the picture.	Er/Sie beschreibt das Bild.
La personne B répond . . .	B replies . . .	B antwortet . . .

CILT

prend une carte . . .	takes a card	nimmt eine Karte . . .
dessine la personne.	draws the person.	zeichnet die Person.
Il faut distribuer les cartes.	You deal the cards.	Man teilt die Karten aus.
Il faut collectionner des familles.	You collect families/sets.	Man sammelt Familien/Sätze.
On va faire deux équipes de	We form 2 teams of	Wir bilden zwei Teams mit
4 garçons et 5 filles.	4 boys and 5 girls.	4 Jungen und 5 Mädchen.
Il faut former un grand cercle.	We'll form a big circle.	Wir machen einen großen Kreis.

17 Changing activity

Ecoutez! Nous allons changer d'activité.	Listen! We are going to change to something else now.	Paßt auf! Wir machen etwas Anderes jetzt.
Quand vous aurez fini/ terminé, on va . . .	When you have finished we will . . .	Wenn ihr fertig seid, werden wir . . .
Vous arrêtez maintenant. Stop!	Stop now.	Halt! Stop! Macht jetzt Schluß!
On passe à autre chose . . .	We are going on to something new.	Wir machen etwas Neues jetzt.
On va chanter/réciter un poème/ répéter/jouer à . . .	We're going to sing/ say a new poem/repeat/play . . .	Wir wollen singen/ein Gedicht aufsagen/wiederholen/ . . . spielen.

18 Ending the lesson

Stop! On va s'arrêter. On arrête.	Stop! We're finishing now.	Stop! Wir machen jetzt Schluß.
La classe est finie.	The bell has gone.	Es hat schon geläutet.
Vite! Ramassez les feuilles/ cahiers/livres/ciseaux . . .	Quickly now, collect the sheets/ exercise books/scissors . . .	Schnell. Sammelt bitte die Blätter/Hefte/Bücher/Scheren . . . ein.
Bon. Rangez vos affaires.	Good. Pack your things away.	Gut. Packt eure Sachen ein.
Un peu de calme , svp!	And let's have quiet now, please!	Und jetzt Ruhe bitte!
Au revoir! A demain!	Goodbye! See you tomorrow!	Auf Wiedersehen! Bis morgen!

19 Playing games (children's phrases)

In order to be able to play simple games in pairs or small groups your pupils will need to learn a small repertoire of key phrases, otherwise they will revert to English immediately and the whole point of the activity is undermined. Here are the basics they will need and you will almost certainly have to teach them this vocabulary by demonstrating how to play each game in front of the whole class with one pupil as your guinea pig/partner.

On y va?	Let's begin.	Fangen wir an?
Tu commences.	You start.	Du beginnst.
C'est à qui?	Whose turn is it?	Wer ist dran?
C'est à toi.	It's your turn.	Du bist dran.
C'est à moi.	It's my turn.	Ich bin dran.
Vas-y!	Go on!	Mach schon!
Donne-moi les cartes.	Give me the cards.	Gib mir die Karten.

Mélange les cartes.	Shuffle the cards.	Misch die Karten.
Distribue les cartes.	Deal the cards.	Teil die Karten aus.
Etale les cartes à l'envers.	Lay the cards face down.	Leg die Karten hin mit dem Gesicht nach unten.
Retourne deux cartes.	Turn over two cards.	Dreh zwei Karten um.
Prends une carte.	Take a card.	Nimm eine Karte.
Collectionne les paires/ une série de . . .	Collect pairs/a set of . . .	Sammel Paare/eine Reihe von . . .
Combien de cartes as-tu?	How many cards have you?	Wie viele Karten hast du?
Pose une carte.	Put a card down.	Leg eine Karte hin.
Lance le dé.	Throw the dice.	Roll den Würfel.
Place ton pion sur une case.	Put your counter on a square.	Leg deinen Spielstein auf ein Feld.
Tourne la toupie.	Spin the spinner.	Dreh den Kreisel.
Le plateau de jeu	games board	Das Spielbrett
Le départ	start	Der Start
L'arrivée	finish	Das Ziel
Avance de deux cases.	Move forward two spaces.	Zwei Felder vorwärts.
Recule de trois cases.	Go back three spaces.	Drei Felder zurück.
Relance le dé.	Throw again.	Noch einmal würfeln.
Passe un tour.	Miss a turn.	Einmal aussetzen.
Le/la gagnant(e)	the winner	Der Sieger
Suzanne a gagné.	Susi won.	Susi hat gewonnen.
J'ai perdu.	I lost.	Ich habe verloren.
J'ai gagné 15 points.	I won 15 points.	Ich habe 15 Punkte gewonnen.

20   Classroom objects

la porte	door	die Tür
la fenêtre	window	das Fenster
le mur	wall	die Wand
l'étagère	bookcase	das Bücherregal
le placard	cupboard	der Schrank
le plancher	floor	der Fußboden
le plafond	ceiling	die Decke
la table	table	der Tisch
la chaise	chair	der Stuhl
le bureau	desk	das Pult
le tableau	board	die Tafel
un essuie-tableau	boardrubber	der Tafelwischer/Schwamm
le chiffon	duster	das Staubtuch
une éponge	sponge	der Schwamm
la craie	chalk	die Kreide
le feutre	felt marker	der Filzstift

le magnétophone	cassette recorder	der Kassettenrecorder
le téléviseur	television set	der Fernseher
le rétroprojecteur	OHP	der Overheadprojektor
le transparent	OHT transparency	die Folie
la vidéo	video	der Videofilm
l'écran	screen	die Leinwand
le calendrier	calendar	der Kalender
le livre	book	das Buch
le cahier	exercise book	das Heft
le classeur	folder/file	die Mappe
le papier	paper	das Papier
le papier-calque	tracing paper	das Pauspapier
le papier à dessin	drawing paper	das Zeichenpapier
le carton	cardboard	der Karton
le crayon	pencil	der Bleistift
le crayon de couleur	crayon	der Buntstift
le taille-crayons	pencil sharpener	der Bleistiftspitzer
la gomme	rubber	der Radiergummi
le stylo	fountain pen	die Feder
le stylo-bille	biro	der Kugelschreiber
le feutre	felt-tip pen	der Filzstift
la règle	ruler	das Lineal
les ciseaux	scissors	die Schere
la colle (le tube)	glue (tube)	der Klebstoff (die Tube)
le scotch	sellotape	das Tesaband
le trombone	paperclip	die Heftklammer
la trousse	pencil case	die Federmappe
le cartable/le sac	schoolbag	die Schultasche

Appendix 2 Common first names

A	*comme*	Alice	Albert		**A**	*wie*	Anna	Adam
B		Béatrice	Bernard		**B**		Beate	Bernd
C		Caroline	Charles		**C**		Carla	Charly
D		Delphine	Denis		**D**		Doris	Dieter
E		Eugénie	Emile		**E**		Elfi	Eugen
F		Florence	Fabrice		**F**		Franziska	Fritz
G		Gisèle	Gérard		**G**		Gisela	Günter
H		Hélène	Henri		**H**		Helga	Helmut
I		Isabelle	Isador		**I**		Ilse	Ignaz
J		Joséphine	Jérôme		**J**		Jutta	Jürgen
K		Karine	Kévin		**K**		Karin	Klaus
L		Laurence	Louis		**L**		Liesl	Ludwig
M		Martine	Michel		**M**		Maria	Manfred
N		Nicolas	Nicole		**N**		Nina	Norbert
O		Olga	Olivier		**O**		Ottilie	Otto
P		Pauline	Pierre		**P**		Petra	Paul
Q			Quentin		**Q**			Quentin
R		Rose	Roger		**R**		Renate	Reinhard
S		Sylvie	Serge		**S**		Susi	Stefan
T		Thérèse	Thomas		**T**		Traude	Thomas
U		Ursula	Ulysse		**U**		Ute	Ulrich
V		Virginie	Vincent		**V**		Veronika	Volker
W			William		**W**		Waltraud	Willi
X		Xavière	Xavier					(Wilhelm)
Y		Yvonne	Yves					
Z		Zoé						

CILT

Appendix 3   Bibliography

BACKGROUND READING FOR TEACHERS

[Items marked with a (p) are aimed specifically at primary teachers.]

Birks R, *Travail d'Instit' - le français de la classe* (Didier/Hatier, 1994) p

Bromidge W and J Burch, *In focus: the languages classroom — learning to communicate* (Video + Teacher's Notes) (CILT, 1993)

3,2,1 . . . Los! (3 videos + Teacher's notes) (KETV, 1996) p

Fernandez S, *Room for two* (NLLIA, 1992) p

Guidelines for Early Foreign Language Learning in Primary schools (Surrey LEA, 1994) p

Halliwell S and B Jones, *On target — teaching in the target language* (CILT, 1992)

Holmes B, *Communication re-activated: teaching pupils with learning difficulties* (CILT, 1991)

Holmes B, *Keeping on target* (CILT, 1994)

Johnstone R, *Teaching modern languages at primary school* (SCRE, 1994) p

MacDonald C, *Using the target language* (ALL/MGP, 1993)

Martin C, *Games and fun activities* (CILT, 1995) p

MLPS — Guidelines (SOED, 1992) p

MLPS — Competences (SOED, 1994) p

MLPS — Advice to teachers (SOED, 1995) p

MLPS — 3 videos of classroom practice (SCOPE/SOED, 1994) p

Modern Foreign Languages in the National Curriculum (SCAA, 1995)

Modern languages in the primary school (MLPS): training packs in French/German (SOED, 1996) p

Phillips S, *Young learners* (OUP, 1993) p

Pilote (3 videos + Teacher's Notes + INSET video) (KETV, 1994) p

Primar: German as FL in primary schools (Journal 3x annually; subscription: Dürr & Kessler/Goethe-Institut) (1992) p

Satchwell P and J de Silva, *Catching them young* (CILT, 1995) p

Target practice (Video + Teacher's Notes) (NCC, 1993)

Tierney D and P Dobson, *Are you sitting comfortably? Telling stories to young language learners* (CILT, 1995) p

RECOMMENDED CLASSROOM RESOURCES FOR TEACHERS OF PRIMARY LANGUAGES

FRENCH

Album des Monstres, *Bevis*	LCP
Bibliobus A and A+ (Graded readers)	MGP
C'est facile comme Bonjour (Resources pack and games pack)	Richmond LEA
Le club (Radio + TV programmes 1994/5)	BBC
Ecoute et chante les lettres, *Jeannot*	Nathan - ESB
ELI Language magazines: Voilà	ELI - ESB
Farandole 1 + 2	Didier/Hatier - ESB
Le francais en chantant	Didier - ESB
Gaston	ELI - ESB
Idées pratiques pour la classe de français	MGP
Jeux faciles and Jeux faciles II, *Cooke*	LCP
Kangarou 1 + 2	Hatier - ESB
Orange bleu, *Beau*	Nathan - ESB
Le petit monde de Pierre (TV fairy-tale)	Ch 4
Les petits Lascars 1–3	Didier/Hatier - ESB
Le petit Trampoline	Clé - ESB
Pilote 1,2,3 (Classroom videos + Teacher's notes)	KETV
Trampoline 1	Clé - ESB
Voilà (Resources pack)	Stanley Thornes

GERMAN

Anna, Schmidt & Oskar 1 (2 videos + P and T bk)	Langenscheidt - ESB
Aurelia 1 (2 cassettes + P + T Bk)	Langenscheidt - ESB
3,2,1 . . . Los! (3 videos + Teacher's notes)	KETV
ELI Language magazines: Fertig-Los! + Kinder	ELI - ESB
Globo TV (Fantasy for beginners)	BBC
Hallo aus Berlin! (TV series for beginners — juniors)	BBC
Huckspack	Klett (UK: Chancerel International)
Ich schreibe über mich	Dürr und Kessler - ESB
Lesekiste A	MGP
Liederkiste (Cassette) Hallo Peter	Kessler - ESB
Praktische Ideen für den Deutschunterricht	MGP
Schatzkiste, *Seeger*	Gilde - ESB
Superspiele I and II (100 photocopiable worksheets)	Cooke LCP

CiLT

Wer?Wie? Was? 1, *Seeger*	Gilde - ESB
Wer/Wie? Was? Lieder machen Spaß, *Wahl*	Gilde - ESB

[ESB = available from European Schoolbooks Ltd, Cheltenham]

NON LANGUAGE-SPECIFIC

Cartoons for Classroom Communication	Miniflashcards
Language Games (various packs with dice and cards)	Miniflashcards
Me, *Brandreth*	Knight Books, Hodder
1000 + Pictures for teachers to copy, *Wright*	Nelson/Longman

IT+WP

European FOLIO
Front Page Europe
Fun with Texts
Pendown
Talking First Word

CD-ROM*

All-in-one Language fun (5 languages)	Syracuse
The cat came back (French/Spanish)	
Goldilocks and the three bears (French/Spanish)	
Kiyeko and the lost night (French,German, Spanish, Italian)	
Mein erstes Lexikon	Dorling Kindersley
Mon premier dictionnaire	Dorling Kindersley
Sitting on the farm (French/Spanish)	
Storybook Weaver Deluxe (French)	
Syracuse Multimedia Language system (French/German/Spanish) (4-9yrs)	
Word Stuff (French/German)	

* All available from Potential Software Ltd, Reigate, Surrey

BOARD AND CARD GAMES + FRENCH/GERMAN PLAY MONEY
available from the European Bookshop, London

Appendix 4 Useful addresses

Central Bureau for Educational Visits and Exchanges (CBEVE)
10 Spring Gardens, London SW1A 2BN

CILT
20 Bedfordbury, London WC2N 4LB

European Bookshop
5 Warwick St, London W1R 6BH

European Schoolbooks Ltd
The Runnings, Cheltenham GL51 9PQ

Mary Glasgow Publications
Ellenborough House, Wellington St, Cheltenham GL50 1YD

Goethe-Institut
50 Princes Gate, London SW7 2PH

Institut français
17 Queensberry Place, London SW7 2DT

KETV/Invicta Media Productions Ltd
74 Middle Deal Road, Deal CT14 9RH

Language Centre Publications
Queensway, Leamington Spa CV31 3JT

Miniflashcards Language Games
PO Box 1526, London W7 1ND

NCET
Milburn Hill Road, Science Park, Coventry CV4 7JJ

Potential Software Ltd
26 Holmesdale Road, Reigate, Surrey RH2 OBQ

SCOPE Picture Productions Ltd
Keppie House, 147 Blythswood St, Glasgow G2 4EN

Scottish CILT
Pathfoot Building, University of Stirling, Stirling FK9 4LA

Scottish Office Education and Industry Department (SOEID)
Victoria Quay, Leith, Edinburgh EH6 6QQ

CiLT